roses

roses

Ludwig Taschner

Struik Publishers
(a division of Struik New Holland Publishing (South Africa) (Pty) Ltd)

80 McKenzie Street
Cape Town 8001
South Africa
www.struik.co.za

New Holland Publishing is a member of the Johnnic Publishing Group

First published in 2000

10 9 8 7 6 5 4 3 2

Copyright © 2000 in published edition:
    Struik Publishers
Copyright © 2000 in text: **Ludwig Taschner**
Copyright © in illustrations: **Georgina Steyn**
Copyright © 2000 in photographs: as credited below

Copyright © of all photographs: **Ludwig Taschner**,
with the exception of the following:
Marianne Alexander: pp. 16-17, 24-25, 40, 41
Nancy Gardiner: pp. 11, 44, 46, 75 (below left),
    100 (top right and bottom)
Struik Image Library/Anthony Johnson; cover, spine,
    pp. 8 (right), 10, 48-49
Zelda Wahl: pp. 30-31

Concept design: **Janice Evans**
Designer: **Lyndall du Toit**
Publishing manager: **Annlerie van Rooyen**
Managing editor: **Lesley Hay-Whitton**
Editor: **Helen de Villiers**

ISBN: 1 86872 400 X

Reproduction by Hirt & Carter Cape (Pty) Ltd
Printed and bound by Times Offset (M) Sdn Bhd

All rights reserved. No part of this publication may be reproduced,
stored in a retrieval system, or transmitted, in any form or by any means,
electronic, mechanical, photocopying, recording or otherwise, without
the prior written permission of the copyright owner(s) or publishers.

Log on to our photographic website www.imagesofafrica.co.za
for an African experience.

CONTENTS

Part One

Federation of Rose Societies 7

Introduction 10

Colours and fragrances 12

Selecting roses by colour and fragrance 14

Contouring and colourscaping 16

Planting procedure 24

Anatomy of a rose 29

Rose care 30

Pest and disease control 40

Growing roses in containers 47

Cut flowers 48

Month-by-month guide to successful rose growing 50

Part Two

Rose growth types 54

Rose family groups 56

Bush roses 60

Floribundas 80

David Austin® English roses & Nostalgia Bush roses 90

Climbers, Ramblers, Shrub and Spire roses 94

David Austin® English roses and Nostalgia Shrubs and Climbers 102

Miniature roses 106

Colourscape roses 113

New roses 119

Index 124

ACKNOWLEDGEMENTS

In the first instance, I would like to pay tribute to the rose for being such an extraordinary teacher and for her stimulating beauty, of which I never tire.

My heartfelt thanks to my wife Pamela and our children, Halmar, Heike and Anja, who have to cope with 'the roses always coming first' in our family life.

Grateful thanks, too, to the 'makers of heavenly roses' – the rose breeders, with whom I am privileged to share this very special feeling for roses; and for being allowed to grow, test and reproduce the best of their varieties in South Africa.

Last, but not least, I acknowledge the on-going incentive to grow more and better roses by being in contact with numerous enthusiastic rosarians in South Africa and many other countries. And I thank the authors of hundreds, even thousands of books, magazines, annuals, newsletters and e-correspondence about roses, published in a language that I can read, who contribute to the art of rose-growing.

LUDWIG TASCHNER

Federation of Rose Societies – R.O.S.A.

P O Box 28165, 0132 Sunnyside Fax 012 544 0813; e-mail *ludwig@ludwigsroses.co.za*

The Rose Society of South Africa was inaugurated in 1961. With the establishment of several regional rose societies, the Federation of Rose Societies of South Africa was launched in 1980 under the chairmanship of Ludwig Taschner. The Federation presently consists of 15 regional societies with a total membership of 3 000. *R.O.S.A. News* is circulated quarterly to all members; and an Annual National Rose Convention is organised. Regional Societies issue their own newsletters, organize rose shows, competitions and visits to parks and gardens, and arrange pruning demonstrations etc.
To become a member, contact ROSA or one of the regional societies listed below.

Boland Roosvereniging
Denise Deetlefs
P O Box 32
De Doorns
6875

Garden Route
Rose Society
Rita Botha
47 Meent Street
George
6529

Goldreef Rose Society
5 Douglas Street
Waverley
Johannesburg
2090

Karoo Roosvereniging
S van Niekerk
P O Box 8
Somerset East
5850

Mpumalanga Roosvereniging
Reinette de Necker
PO Box 3206
Secunda
2302

Natal Midlands Rose Society
Debbie Battershill
PO Box 20151
Ashburton
3200

Natal Rose Society
Ken Braum
2 Sylvan Close
Umhlanga Rocks
4320

Northern Natal Rose Society
Nila Dannhauser
PO Box 1395
Vryheid
3100

Northern Rose Society
Ludwig Taschner
PO Box 28188
Sunnyside
0132

Vrystaatse Roosvereniging
Anneke Brits
PO Box 100644
Renosterspruit
9326

Western Cape Rose Society
Billy Hendricks
15 Glencarol Way
Glenhaven
Bellville
7530

part one

how to grow roses

Introduction

One of the many sayings about the most romantic of all flowers is 'A rose is a rose is a rose'. The reality is not as simple as that: the versatility of roses lies not only in their huge variety of colours and tints, but also in the extensive range of flower shapes and sizes and multiple growth forms.

Roses have graced our planet for at least 30 million years. The origins of the rose are widespread – from the humid climate of China to the hot, dry, desert conditions of the middle East, and from the moderate environment of Europe and north America to freezing Alaska. Today, some 50 000 different rose varieties are grown all over the world.

Roses are inextricably linked to romance, as many of their names suggest: 'Fair Bianca', 'Ivory Beauty', 'Bride's Dream', 'L'Aimant' and 'String of Pearls'. Roses are noble flowers too, their names often reflecting loved or eminent people in whose honour particular varieties have been created, such as 'My Granny', 'Caroline de Monaco', 'Maria Callas', 'Vivaldi', and, of course, our very own 'Madiba'. Throughout the ages, roses have been entwined in coats of arms and woven into legends and fairy tales.

Colour remains the guiding principle in selecting roses; it is the source of many arguments between couples who visit garden centres. I would possibly never have become as passionate about roses had my entry into specialized horticulture not coincided with the creation of orange roses. 'Super Star' was extraordinary in its time, and even today, my eyes are drawn to an orange rose first of all.

No advice or statement in gardening must be seen as being written in stone. Every garden has its very own microclimate and unique soil structure, and your gardening practice is bound to be different from that of your neighbour, and with different results. Although this book focuses on rose growing in southern Africa, it will obviously also apply to other countries in both hemispheres with similar subtropical climatic conditions.

WHY GROW ROSES?

Flowering rose plants on display at garden centres are often bought on impulse. But there are other compelling and enduring reasons for planting roses:

As a source of cut flowers

The image of a huge bowl of roses inspires many people to plant roses in their garden. Hybrid Tea roses, which usually produce a profusion of flowering stems, with one bud per stem, are by far the most popular. Other varieties that also provide an array of good cut flowers are Floribundas, English roses, Miniatures, Climbers and Groundcover roses. For more information on this topic, see the chapter 'Cut flowers', on page 48.

To provide colour

Modern roses are able to flower virtually continuously for six to twelve months of the year, colouring our gardens and our lives with an abundance and variety that is virtually unparalleled in the flower kingdom. The great variation in growth patterns allows for selecting varieties that give colour at different heights, and particularly at eye level; descriptions of rose varieties (in Part Two of this book) indicate the colour, height and growth pattern of each rose. See the chapter 'Colours and fragrances', starting on page 12.

For their scent

The fragrance of roses is legendary. Roses in antiquity were grown as much for their scent as for their beauty – today, with the proliferation of rose varieties, the choice is that much wider. In ancient Greece, rose oil (attar) was obtained by steeping fragrant rose petals in oil.

Rosewater is produced by mixing a few drops of rose attar in a litre of distilled water. Its value in distant times is evidenced by the record of an ancient transaction: between 810 and 817, the government treasury in Baghdad demanded a tribute of 30 000 flasks of rosewater from a nearby province which had mastered the production of both attar and rosewater. See the chapter 'Colours and fragrances', starting on page 12.

CONDITIONS THAT SUIT ROSES
Temperature
Roses can withstand a wide range of temperatures. In general, hot, dry conditions are preferable to humid conditions. Roses adopt winter dormancy when temperatures fall below zero at night and less than 10°C in the day. With minimum night temperatures of 10°C and correspondingly warmer temperatures of 18°C to 25°C during the day, roses will happily flower non-stop for 12 months of the year, providing they have been watered, fertilized and groomed as required.

Light
Roses require considerable light to be able to flower. Their flowering ability is reduced in direct proportion to reduced light. Sufficient light can mean either intensive light on shorter days, or more diffuse light as found in Europe on long days under an overcast sky. To flower freely, roses require direct light for about five hours in the morning when planted east of a building, or in the afternoon when planted west of a building. In situations with less than four hours of direct light, fewer flowers will be produced.

Soil types
The condition of the soil can always be adjusted to suit roses. Sandy clay is ideal, as it offers good aeration as well as water retention. To improve plain clay, add sand, gravel or coarse organic material; and to upgrade sandy soil, add water-retaining materials such as peat moss or other organic matter. Lime can be added to acidic soil and flower of sulphur to alkaline soil to achieve the desired, neutral pH. Read about soil preparation in the chapter 'Planting procedure', on page 24.

Watering
Although roses are 'water wise' and able to adjust to the quantity of water available, they cannot generate new stems and flowers during the growing season without regular watering. The broad, basic requirement is 10 litres per plant per week. This varies according to the size of the plant and the condition of the soil. Take a more detailed look at watering in 'Rose care' on page 30.

Containers
Roses grow and flower well in most types and sizes of pots or containers, particularly the free-flowering Colourscape varieties. For more details, read the chapter 'Growing roses in containers' on page 47.

Colours and fragrances

Colour and fragrance in flowers originally served to tempt insect life – and so ensured the survival of the species. But the siren song of the rose has, over the aeons, captured a far wider audience. In a fitting tribute to the species, the image of a fragrant, red rose has become the universal symbol of love.

THOUGHTS ON COLOUR

The full colour spectrum is found in sunlight – ranging from red, orange, yellow, green, blue and indigo, through to violet. These spectral colours run into each other, creating an infinitely vast and varied range of tints.

The colour of blooms and foliage depends on the three main pigments found in each plant cell. Chloroplast is the carrier of green, or chlorophyll. These pigments, concentrated in the leaves, absorb sunlight and carbon dioxide, which they process into sugar, providing nourishment and energy. Leucoplast pigments are carriers of yellow and white, while chromoplast is the carrier of red, orange and yellow pigments.

Further variations are brought about by a layer of wax (cuticula) on the epidermis that reflects light and makes the petals shine like silk. Other petals have an uneven surface that diffuses the light, and their appearance is velvety. Absorbed light in a flower brings about further chemical reaction, resulting in changing colours as the bud opens, blooms, and then fades.

How colour affects mood

Although everyone evaluates colours independently, it has been found that intense observation of a colour can influence our body chemistry.

Red is the strongest emotional colour, the colour of love and also of danger. Intense observation of red can cause a release of adrenaline, which triggers alertness and feelings of stress. Large beds of red roses are superb in open parks, but red can be a difficult colour if used intensively in a small garden.

Stress-reducing green results from a balanced mixture of yellow and blue. Scientific research in the 1950s found that surroundings of green were least tiring for the eyes.

THE SYMBOLIC VALUES OF COLOUR

Red ◆	the colour of blood, represents love;
Blue ◆	shows trust when one is far away;
Yellow ◆	denotes jealousy and envy;
Green ◆	stands for nature, youth and hope;
White ◆	represents purity

Many offices and working environments were painted green, until it was found that too much green leads to monotony and lack of attention. That is why parks and gardens must be enlivened with colourful flowers to retain our interest.

Blue is the colour of distance and the horizon, of Heaven and of the Earth. It is the colour of never-ending desire. Blue flowers planted at the periphery of a garden give the impression of increased space.

Yellow is the colour of confident, happy, lively people. This colour loosens the mood and signals energy. Just as blue flowers in a garden appear to increase its size, yellow flowers are planted to shorten distances. Yellow comes forward to viewers – blue moves away.

Orange combines the strength of red with the cheer of yellow. It denotes energy and pride, but also passion. German poet and natural scientist Johann Wolfgang von Goethe wrote '. . . it is not surprising that energetic, healthy and robust people enjoy this colour the most'.

Purple-violet is the colour of power. It is a mixture of cold blue

THOUGHTS ON SCENTED ROSES

Throughout the ages, man has sought to capture the tantalisingly elusive perfume of the rose. People seem instinctively to bow to a rose bloom – its beauty is a lure that holds the promise of further delight. One inhales deeply, eyes closed to focus the senses and, if the rose proves to be fragrant, ecstasy ensues!

It is a common belief that modern roses have lost the powerful fragrance of older varieties. In fact, most fragrant old rose varieties are still being grown today. What is more, most modern roses are superior in flowering ability, brightness of colour, shape of flower and firmness of petal.

Some 25 different sorts of rose scents can be identified and some roses have a mixture of these perfumes. Most Hybrid Teas appear to contain seven of the basic scents associated with the genus, or a mixture of them: rose, nasturtium, oris, violet, apple, lemon and clover.

To identify rose perfume:

Begin with a brief sniff, no more than a few seconds long, lest the hypersensitive nasal olfactory cells become anaesthetized. Let your memory go to work. Explore your personal collection of scents for a similar fragrance. Having analysed the head space, take a deeper sniff and smell the heart and then the base of the rose. (Remember that it takes 12 hours for a rose to play all its notes, and the composition of smells varies during the day.)

On average, people are able to memorise and identify several hundred different smells. Henri Delbard, in *A Passion for Roses*, appends colours to scents and allocates a pyramid of colours to each variety. Since scent is generated when alcohol oxidises, temperature plays a major role in the release of perfume. On warm days, fragrance is strongest. During cold spells, fragrant varieties may lose all trace of their perfume; while extreme heat can cause fragrance to escape faster than it is made.

It is futile to pick an immature bud and peal off its petals to establish its scent. In this respect, the rose differs from many other flowers. The oils in a rose can only be synthesized by mature cells at a relatively late stage. Cut roses from florists may have no fragrance as they are often harvested at an immature stage. Blooms picked when the outer petals have fully reflected will exude perfume for days to come at evenly warm room temperature.

The scent comes from tiny cells on the undersides of the petals. As a rule, dark-coloured roses are more strongly scented than those of lighter hue. Cross-pollination, however, is changing the rules, resulting in varieties of strongly scented white roses – and deep-red blooms with hardly any fragrance at all.

Some categories of scents:
- citrus
- aromatics, such as aniseed and lavender
- flora, such as rose, jasmine and lilac
- greenery
- fruit, such as raspberry, pear and peach
- spices, which include cloves, nutmeg and cinnamon
- wood and balsam i.e. vanilla and heliotrope at the base.

and hot red. An important symbolic colour of the Catholic church, it denotes penance, seclusion, transgression, acceptance of destiny, and also desire. Planted in small patches in a garden this colour can create an unforgettable impression, but in large areas can seem threatening.

White roses are 'noble'. White is the colour of innocence, of the virgin bride and of peace. White flowers signify mourning and death, and are often used for coffin decoration. When touched, a snowflake melts; white rose petals, when touched, turn brown. That is why white is considered to be a metaphysical colour – it is untouchable.

Pastel colours free endorphins, the 'happy makers' in our brains. In surroundings of entirely soft, pastel colours, feelings of wellbeing tend to fade unless small quantities of other colours are introduced to create the variety necessary for longer-lasting feelings of contentment.

> To test for fragrance, pick a semi-open bloom and keep it in your pocket or under your hat for half an hour. You will soon know whether it is a fragrant variety or not.

Colours and fragrances   13

Selecting roses by colour and fragrance

TYPE	red	pink	yellow	copper	mauve	creamy	tinted
HYBRID TEAS	Alec's Red Boksburg Fantasia Cora Marie Red 'n Fragrant Five Roses Ingrid Bergman Mister Lincoln Mother's Value Oklahoma	New Zealand Andrea Stelzer Anna Belami Marijke Koopman Bewitched Bride's Dream Electron Esther Geldenhuys Garden Queen Lisa Pink Crinolene Queen Elizabeth Rina Hugo Shaleen Surtie-Richards Summer Lady	Casanova Egoli Germiston Gold Golden Monika Johannesburg Sun Moon Adventure	Coppertone Just Joey Lovers' Meeting Durbanville Flame Monika Tanned Beauty Vera Johns Janine Herholdt Belle Epoque	Burning Sky Blue Moon Madiba Pridwin Spiced Coffee Super Bowl Zulu Royal	Elina Leana Memoire Pascali Virginia	Beach Girl Brigadoon Double Delight Hanneli Rupert Modern Art Mondiale Peace Peace of Vereeniging Sheila's Perfume Warm Wishes Yankee Doodle
FLORIBUNDAS	Bavaria City of Belfast Little Red Hedge Mathias Meilland Satchmo Striking	Bienkie Bridget Colchester Beauty Carefree Wonder Sandton Smile Flower Power Karoo Rose Manou Meilland Pernille Poulsen Simplicity Springs '75 St. Andrew's	Collegiate 110 Friesia Goldmarie Gold Reef Strilli	Fellowship My Estelle Huguenot 300 Orange Sensation Playboy	Blue Bayou Shocking Blue®	Iceberg Ivory Beauty St John Nonacentenary Summer Snow	Durban July Nicole Pearl of Bedfordview S O S Children's Rose Rainbow Nation Zola Budd
MINIATURES	Maidy Red Rosamini Red Shadows Zinger	Cupcake Figurine Jennifer Joy Peach Festival Pierine String of Pearls	Gee Gee® Good Morning America Rise 'n Shine	Denver's Dream Ocarina® Teddy Bear Starina Fall Festival Picaninni	Lavender Jade Raindrops Winsome	Amoretta® Pacesetter Party Girl Spearmint	Anita Charles Autumn Magic Chasin' Rainbow Magic Carousel® Minnie Pearl Rainbow's End Sweet Symphony Zephelene
CLIMBERS	Altissimo® Don Juan Iskra Olive Tradescant	Blossom Magic Blossom Time Clair Matin Rose Celeste Galway Bay Salmon Spire® Heritage Mary Rose	Aperitif Casino Golden Showers Golden Celebration	Amber Spire Kordes Brilliant Pat Austin Abraham Darby Jude the Obscure Crepuscule Coral Midinette Apricot Midinette	Lavender Midinette	Great North Iceberg White Spire Swan Softee	Double Delight Handel Joseph's Coat Sutter's Gold Tullamore Isidingo

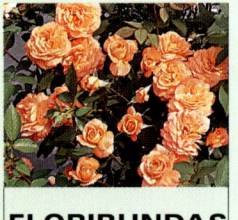

Colours and fragrances

ENGLISH NOSTALGIA	red	pink	yellow	copper	mauve	creamy	tinted
Bush Roses	L D Braithwaite Francois Krige The Prince	Addo Heritage Magaliesburg Roos Adele Searll Sharifa Wife of Bath		Ambridge Rose Helpmekaar Roos L'Aimant Troilus	Charles Rennie Mackintosh Prospero	Fair Bianca Glamis Castle Joan Kruger	
Shrub Roses	The Squire	Ballerina Betty Prior Gwen Fagan Margaret Roberts	Molineux	Kordes Brilliant		Candida Winchester Cathedral	
Standard Roses	Alec's Red	Belami	Germiston Gold	Brigadoon	Burning Sky	Caroline de Monaco	Chicago Peace

Hybrid Tea	Black Madonna
	Five Roses
	Ingrid Bergman
	Oklahoma
	Samourai
		Electron
		Marijke Koopman
		New Zealand
		Shaleen Surtie-
		  Richards
		Summer Lady
		Bewitched
		Duet
			Egoli
			Harry Oppenheimer
				Belle Epoque
				Coppertone
				Duftwolke
				Harmonie
				Just Joey
				Tanned Beauty
				Warm Wishes
					Blue Moon
					Spiced Coffee
					Super Bowl
					Pridwin
						Elina
						Leana
						Memoire
						Virginia
							Caribbean
							Hanneli Rupert
							Peace of
							  Vereeniging
							Southern Sun
							Technikon Pretoria

Floribunda	Bavaria
	City of Belfast
	Mathias Meilland
	Satchmo
	Lava Glow
		Colchester Beauty
		Flower Power
		Karoo Rose
		Pernille Poulsen
		Simplicity
		St Andrew's
		Johannesburg
		  Garden Club
		Playgirl
		Manou Meilland
			Friesia
			Goldmarie
			Gold Reef
			Strilli
			Gold Bunny
				Fellowship
				Courvoisier
				Huguenot 300
				Orange Sensation
					Blue Bayou
					Shocking Blue®
						Iceberg
						Summer Snow
							City of Pretoria
							Durban July
							Nicole
							Pearl of
							  Bedfordview
							Rainbow Nation

SELECTED FRAGRANT ROSES

Hybrid Tea		Floribunda	Nostalgia	Miniatures
Alec's Red	New Zealand	Bavaria	Adele Searll	Lavender Jade
Belle Epoque	Oklahoma	Bella Rosa	Fair Bianca	Pacesetter
Bewitched	Oyster Pearl	Colchester Beauty	Glamis Castle	Picaninni
Blue Moon	Pascali	Courvoisier	L'Aimant	Winsome
Casanova	Pridwin	Elizabeth of Glamis	Sharifa	
Double Delight	Red 'n Fragrant	Flower Power	The Prince	
Duftwolke	Sheila's Perfume	Friesia	Troilus	
Electron	Super Bowl	Manou Meilland	Wife of Bath	
Just Joey	Tanned Beauty	Sandton Smile		
Marijke Koopman	Warm Wishes	Shocking Blue		
Mister Lincoln	Garden Queen	St Andrew's		

Colours and fragrances 15

Contouring and colourscaping

Roses are often simply planted in any available sunny or semi-sunny spot in the garden, with no sense of grouping. Obviously, garden layout or grouping (whether by colour or growth pattern) has no influence on the performance of roses, but a well-thought-out arrangement can greatly enhance their impact. With this in mind, take a good look around your garden. Where is colour required, and at what height?

MODERN GARDEN DESIGN

The driveway from the street to the carport often has a confined space on one side, possibly a wall or fence to the neighbour's property. If this area needs livening up with colour, roses would be well suited to the task. A good choice would be Spire roses, which are narrow but tall-growing, with compact roses in front of them. Alternatively, in more confined spaces, Standard roses would be suitable, spaced at 1 m to 1,5 m, with two Bush roses between every two Standards. Where this latter combination is chosen, all the Standard roses could be of one colour (the white Floribunda 'Iceberg' would be particularly spectacular here, as it is such an excellent performer) and contrasting or mixed colours at the lower level or the other way around, with mixed colours as Standards and a uniform colour below. The same combination could be repeated on the other side of the driveway. This planting arrangement defines the driveway and still allows a view into the rest of the front garden.

Another obvious place for planting roses is just outside the wall or fence to one's property. Security has forced these walls upon us, and a suitable selection of roses planted on the street side breaks the monotony, makes the property more friendly looking – and adds to security. Shrub and Climbing roses with a spreading growth habit and low maintenance requirements are most suitable here.

Walls on the north, east and west faces of the house are often asking to be enlivened with roses. With root systems that in no way endanger house foundations, roses can be planted close to the wall (50 cm away). Alternatively, if a path runs next to the wall, roses can be

Standard and Bush rose layout for confined spaces

planted next to the path. Varieties should be selected that will not obstruct the view from windows into the garden, but that enhance the view of the house from the garden. Hybrid Tea roses are a logical choice: it places them conveniently close to the house for picking blooms.

The colour of the house walls will influence the choice of rose colour, as well as those colours most desired for indoor decoration. Additional height can be achieved with Standard roses or tall-growing Hybrid Tea varieties for the spaces between windows (see illustration below). These flowerbeds need not be confined to narrow spaces or straight rows, but can follow the informal landscape contours of the garden. In this case, even low-growing roses such as the Sunsation range or Miniatures can be planted in the foreground. Again, if a mixture of colours is chosen for the Hybrid Tea roses, a border row of uniformly coloured roses unites the design.

A wall of colour can be achieved on the inside boundary wall or fence. Start by planting Climbing roses next to a high wall or fence. About 2 m inside, plant a row of Spire roses, and in front of these, spaced at about 1-m intervals, a row of tall Hybrid Tea varieties. Allow a wider space of 2 m for a working path before the next row of medium-height Hybrid Teas, and then a row of compact-growing Floribundas or Sunsation roses. This last row could be contoured to fit in with a softer, scalloped layout to the general landscape. If space is limited, start with a row of Spire roses, followed by a row of medium-height Hybrid Teas; then leave a narrow path of 1,5 m and plant a row of compact roses and a row of Miniatures or very prostrate Groundcover roses in front of them.

Sometimes small groupings of Hybrid Tea or Floribunda roses are desired, perhaps in front of taller evergreen shrubs or free-standing

Using spaces between windows

Contouring and colourscaping 17

in the lawn. Three or four rose plants can be placed in one large hole, or planted in separate, closely grouped holes. Usually one would plant several bushes of the same variety – but you can 'cheat' by planting different varieties, making visitors wonder at the range of colours achieved on a 'single' bush. Winter pruning of such a grouping should proceed as normal – but leave up to eight stems instead of the normal three or four.

In large, park-like gardens it is particularly gratifying to play with colour schemes. The garden can be divided into sections, each representing a single colour reflected by all the shrubs and trees in that section. For instance, if one section is restricted to pink blooms of all types, the next section could display just reds or yellows or oranges, setting up surprise vistas for viewers.

Colourscape roses – varieties with an unusual, spreading growth pattern – lend themselves to many different uses. Miniature Climbers look good on pool fences; Shrub roses form medium-high hedges for screening off certain parts of the garden; trailing Groundcover roses can be planted on top of retention walls or embankments; Umbrella Standards make interesting features; Ramblers look good over pergolas, arches or poles; and Colourscape varieties make excellent container shrubs.

Sunsation roses are increasingly replacing bedding plants to create permanent, colourful borders. The name 'Sunsation', coined with modern marketing in mind, implies a sensation in the sun. Sunsation roses are groundcover roses with a prostrate growth habit that flower almost continuously during the growing season. They are hardy and require very low maintenance.

Fiery Sunsation roses

VICTORIAN ROSE GARDEN DESIGNS

Garden design and layout have undergone many changes over the years, but formal gardens, particularly rose gardens, can still be seen in many parks, mostly in Europe. And formal design still shapes many private gardens, even within a larger, less formal structure.

Eclectic Victorian landscape design made use of roses in every form, whether climbing, shrub or bush. Design revolved around objects set in space, rather than shaping of spaces themselves.

The Victorian house stood prominently apart, with no plants linking it to the garden – quite the opposite of today's trend, where outdoor space is an extension of indoor living.

Today, landscapers can draw on Victorian design ideas to enhance modern layouts. It is not necessary to adopt an entire design, or to remodel an existing garden, but rather to make use of Victorian design principles to help create features in our parks and gardens.

These are the design principles:
- The design is usually symmetrical, with straight or curved lines based on geometric forms.
- Paths are located on one or more axes.
- Beds, lawns and pools are geometrically shaped.
- Columns, arches and trelliswork are used to emphasize the design.
- Classical ornaments and statues are used as focal points.
- Brick or paved courtyards are incorporated in the design.
- Topiary plants are clipped and shaped into columns, balls, spirals, pyramids and cones, and used as focal points.

Six general design rules were followed

1 The principal structure on the site was to be the dominant visual element, with other features designed to maximise the structure's scale and ornateness.
2 All lines and forms were exaggerated both in layout and detailing.
3 Forms used were realistic, rather than abstract.
4 Details from foreign historical styles were incorporated.
5 The ground plane was the most significant surface.
6 Individual features were isolated visually and physically.

If you decide on a Victorian-design rose bed, you must be prepared to spend time maintaining, cutting and grooming the roses on a very regular basis.

The colour wheel is still the most popular Victorian design. Although tall roses were originally selected to screen the surprise element of the inner circle, this is not essential. Colour-wheel roses can just as easily be of an even height, with only the centre feature standing proud. Or roses can be selected to form a pyramid, with very low varieties on the outer edge, changing gradually to taller varieties. The same applies to the square and square walk-about designs. To reverse the pyramid effect, with tall plants on the outer edge, simply reverse planting of the selected varieties.

Red was the dominant colour in Victorian times, but nowadays we can choose from the full spectrum of colours. (The Victorians did not have the very brilliant red, orange, bright yellow and two-toned roses that we have today.) Or you could restrict colour to just pastel shades; contrast soft with bright colours; or just use bright colours.

See the following sketches for design ideas and suggestions of rose varieties used in formal designs.

COLOUR WHEEL DESIGN

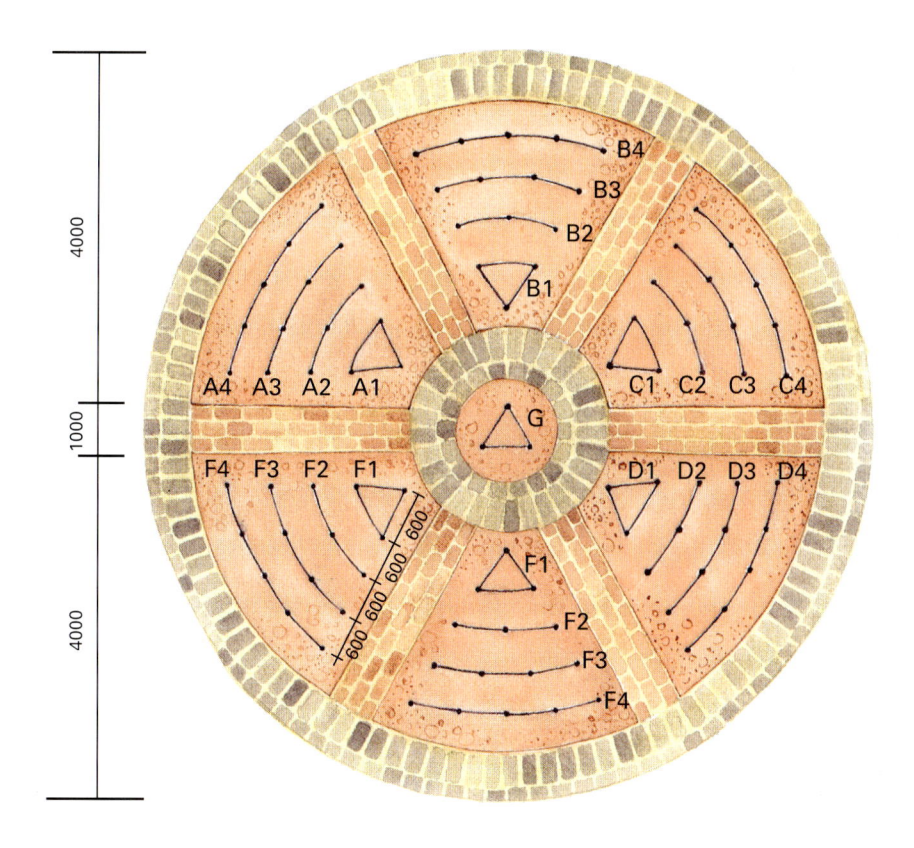

Suggested rose varieties for the Colour Wheel design:

A1	Friesia
A2	Bright Smile
A3	Goldmarie '82
A4	Princess Alice
B1	Blue Bayou
B2	Shocking Sky
B3	Shocking Blue®
B4	Mauve Melodee
C1	Pernille Poulsen
C2	Flower Power
C3	Simplicity
C4	Carefree Wonder
D1	Playboy
D2	Fellowship
D3	City of Pretoria
D4	Peace Keeper
E1	Mathias Meilland
E2	City of Belfast
E3	Glowing Achievement
E4	Satchmo
F1	Orange Bunny
F2	Orange Sensation
F3	Orange Sparkle
F4	Oudtshoorn Joy
G	Iceberg

This 'Colour Wheel' is a basic plan that can be changed according to personal taste. 'Colour Wheels' are ideal for compartmentalizing colours. These can flow from light to deep shades, or each wedge can contrast with its neighbours. All the roses can be of a similar height, offering a sweeping view of the full colour display; or, starting from the outside with low-growing roses, plants of increasing size can be used towards the centre, creating a pyramid effect. Alternatively, it is possible to create privacy by selecting tall varieties for the periphery, and moving towards lower-growing varieties in the centre.

Contouring and colourscaping

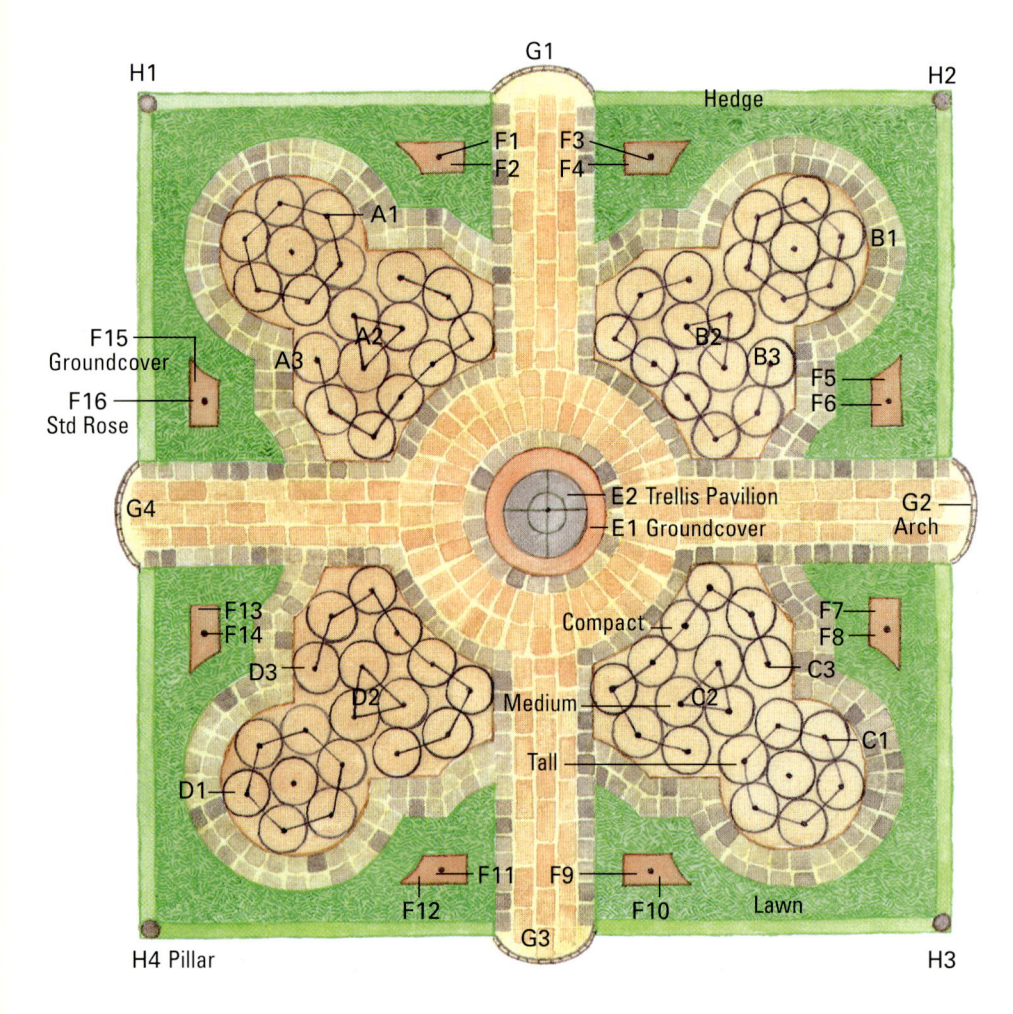

SQUARE WALK-ABOUT DESIGN

Suggested rose varieties for the 'Square Walk-about' design:

A1	Springs '75
A2	St Andrew's
A3	Bridget
B1	Colchester Beauty
B2	Bridal Pink
B3	Georgie Girl
C1	Springs '75
C2	St Andrew's
C3	Bridget
D1	Colchester Beauty
D2	Bridal Pink
D3	Georgie Girl
E1	Pink Sunsation
E2	Iceberg (Climber)
F1	Iceberg (STD)
F3	Iceberg (STD)
F6	Iceberg (STD)
F8	Iceberg (STD)
F9	Iceberg (STD)
F11	Iceberg (STD)
F14	Iceberg (STD)
F16	Iceberg (STD)
F2	Alyssum 'Snow Crystal'
F4	Alyssum 'Snow Crystal'
F5	Alyssum 'Snow Crystal'
F7	Alyssum 'Snow Crystal'
F10	Alyssum 'Snow Crystal'
F12	Alyssum 'Snow Crystal'
F13	Alyssum 'Snow Crystal'
F15	Alyssum 'Snow Crystal'
G1	New Dawn
G2	Compassion
G3	New Dawn
G4	Compassion
H1	Felicia
H2	Fellemberg
H3	Penelope
H4	Cornelia

This design could be placed in the centre of a large lawn, in full view of the house, or at the end of the garden close to the fence or wall. Use your imagination to select colour groupings and differing heights, as well as the material used for paving and edging.

Contouring and colourscaping

SQUARE DESIGN

Suggested rose varieties for the 'Square' design:

A1	Magaliesburg Roos
A2	Bridal Pink
A3	Georgie Girl
A4	Ambridge Rose
B1	Springs '75
B2	St Andrew's
B3	Bridget
B4	Simplicity
C1	Magaliesburg Roos
C2	Bridal Pink
C3	Georgie Girl
C4	Ambridge Rose
D1	Springs '75
D2	St Andrew's
D3	Bridget
D4	Simplicity
E1	My Granny (STD)
E2	String of Pearls

Alternative suggestion:

A1	Coral Spire
A2	Iceberg
A3	Salmon Sunsation®
A4	Lisa
A5	Rosy Cheeks
A6	Salmon Spire®
A7	Iceberg
A8	Salmon Sunsation®
B1	My Granny (STD)
B2	Cupcake
C1	Coral Spire
C2	Iceberg
C3	Salmon Sunsation®
C4	Lisa
C5	Rosy Cheeks
C6	Salmon Spire®
C7	Iceberg
C8	Salmon Sunsation®

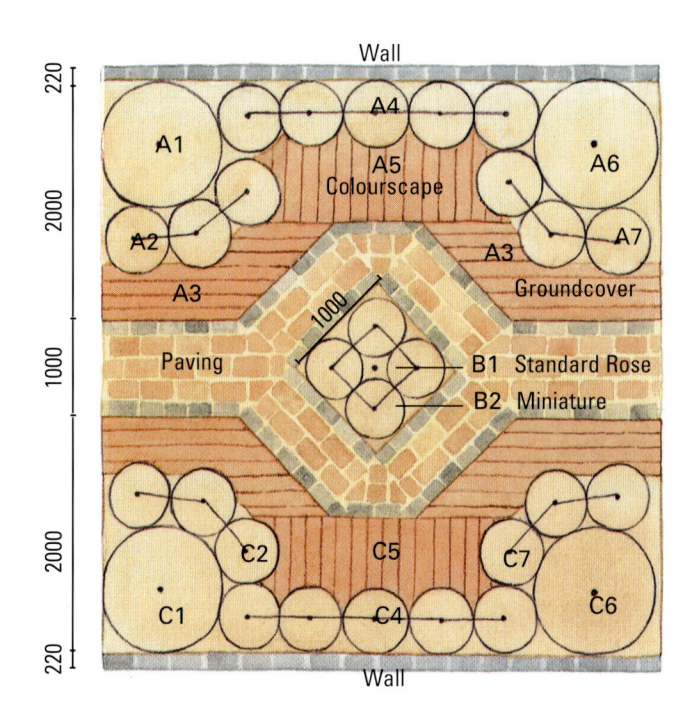

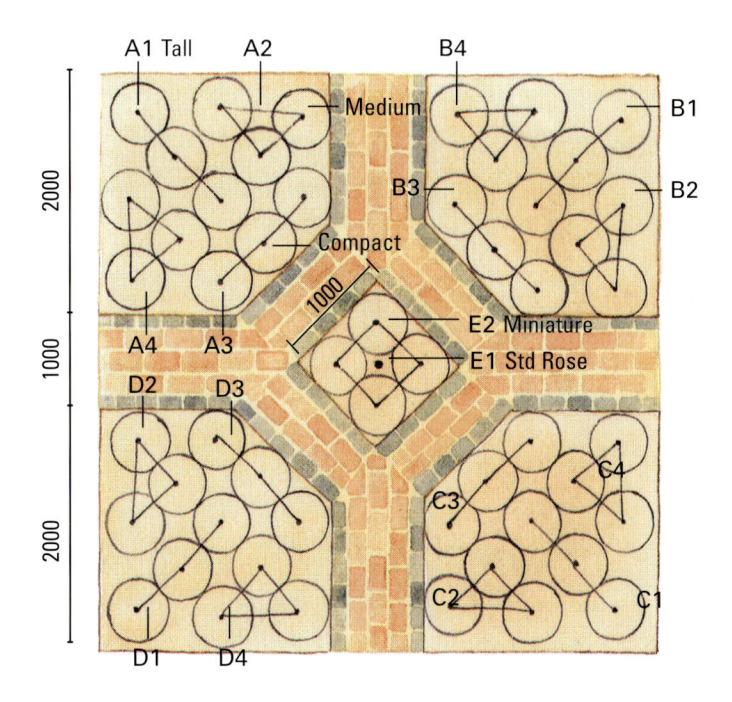

These two design patterns give an idea of how a confined space can be utilized to the maximum.

Contouring and colourscaping

CORNER DESIGN

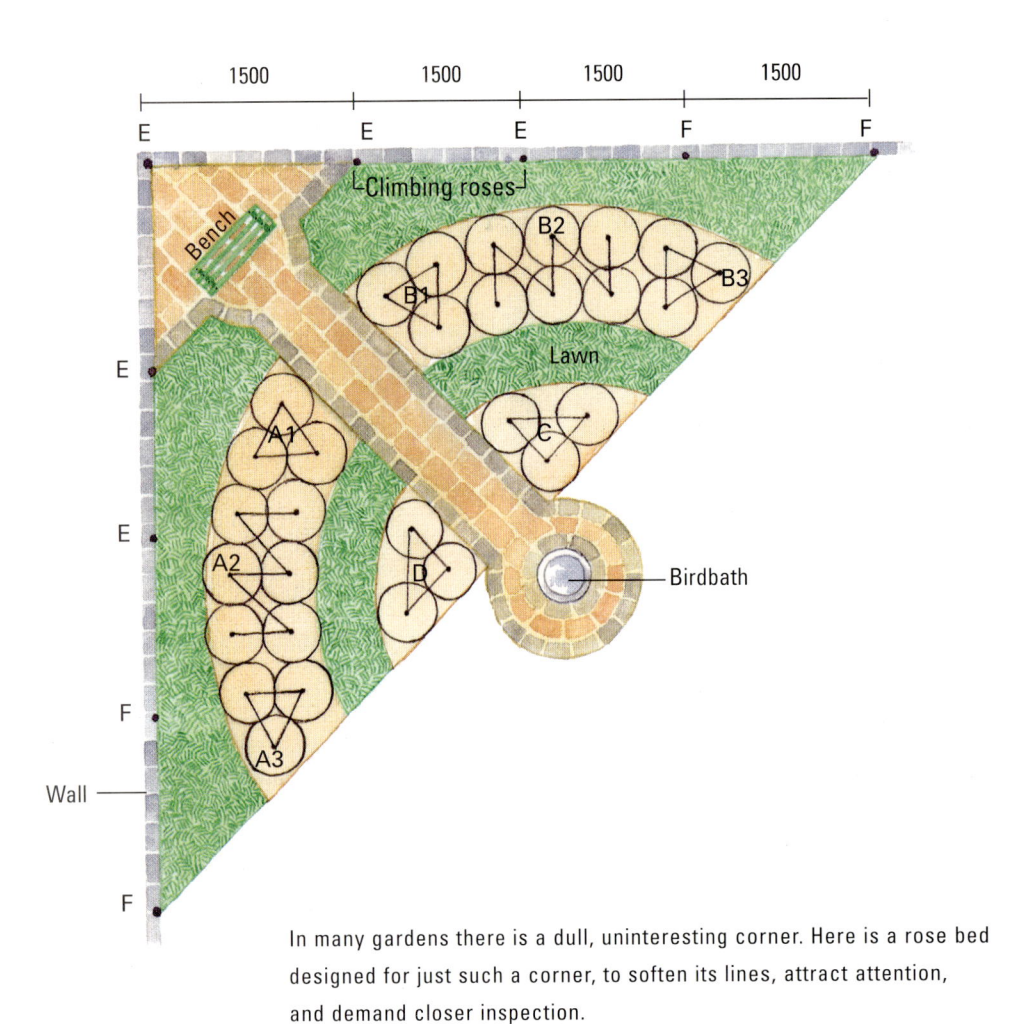

Suggested rose varieties for the 'Corner' design:

Example 1

A1	Huguenot 300
A2	Bridal Pink
A3	Elizabeth of Glamis
B1	Huguenot 300
B2	Bridal Pink
B3	Elizabeth of Glamis
C	Georgie Girl
D	Coral Palace
E	Great North
F	Coral Spire

Example 2

A1	Prospero
A2	Mary Rose
A3	Magaliesburg Roos
B1	Prospero
B2	Mary Rose
B3	Magaliesburg Roos
C	Sharifa
D	Glamis Castle
E	Heritage
F	Swan

In many gardens there is a dull, uninteresting corner. Here is a rose bed designed for just such a corner, to soften its lines, attract attention, and demand closer inspection.

TRIANGLES IN A SQUARE

See plan top of page 23

22 Contouring and colourscaping

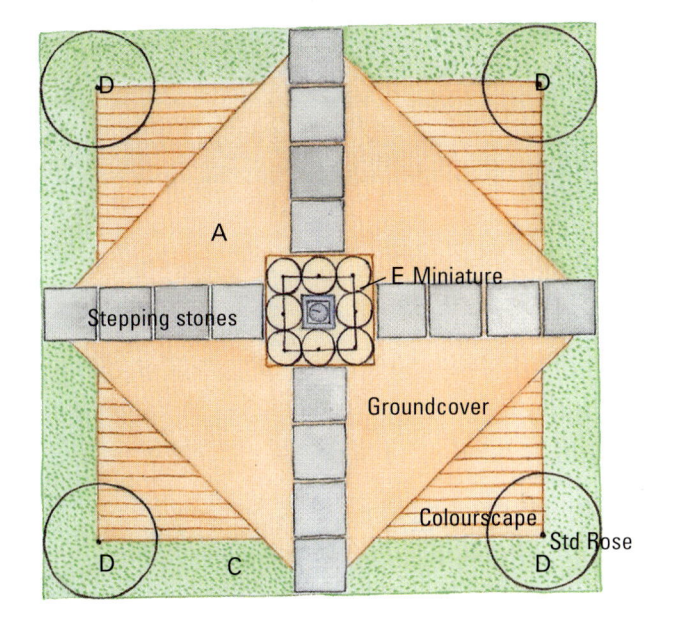

Suggested rose varieties for the 'Triangles in a Square' design:
A   White Sunsation
B   Fiery Sunsation
C   Mentha Pulgeium
    (Penny Royal - mint)
D   Iceberg (STD)

An interesting design variation within a square, in which one can experiment with colours and heights.

OVAL DESIGN

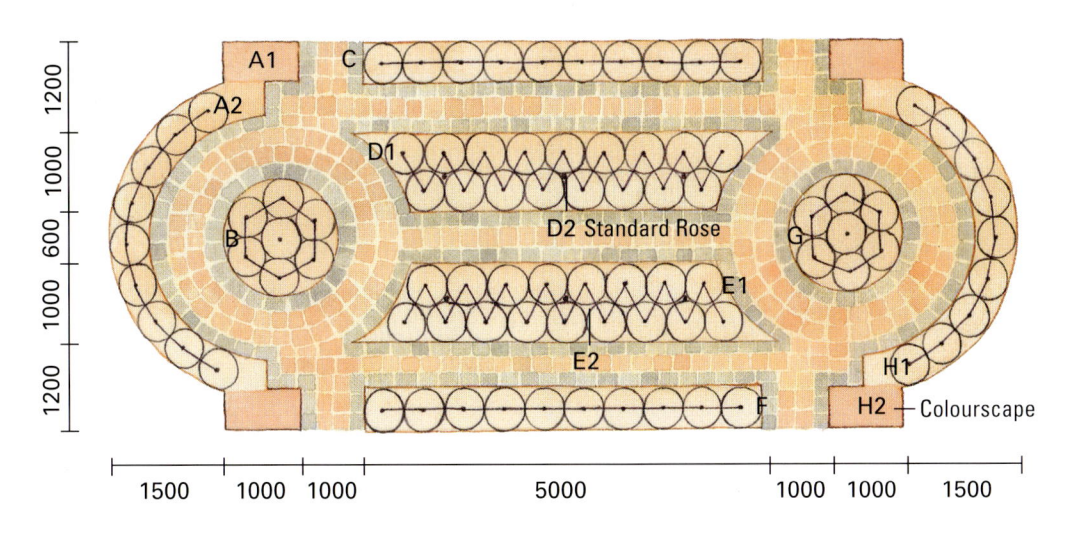

Suggested rose varieties for the 'Oval' design:

A1   Summer Snow
A2   Iceberg
B   Bright Smile
C   Iceberg
D1   Friesia
D2   Iceberg (STD)
E1   Friesia
E2   Iceberg (STD)
F1   Iceberg
G   Gold Reef
G1   Iceberg
H2   Summer Snow

An oval bed can be constructed in front of a shrubbery in a large garden; close to a fence or border wall or next to a tennis court enclosure; or length-wise as a partial division in the lawn. The layout suggests a selection of showy Floribundas and Hybrid Teas, which would ensure a good supply of cut flowers for the home.

Contouring and colourscaping   23

Planting procedure

The planting procedure followed will determine the future of your roses; it will establish their potential to flourish – or set the scene for failure. Preparation of soil, size of hole and extent of aftercare depend very much on a range of factors: on the existing condition of the ground, the nature of the terrain and the prevailing climatic and weather conditions. Bear in mind too that bare-rooted roses require different treatment from those established in containers. The following planting advice is specifically for roses established in containers.

SOIL PREPARATION

Roses grow in almost any type of soil, but the pH, alkalinity or acidity of the soil most suitable for roses is neutral (pH 6,5), or slightly acidic.

To achieve this condition, add agricultural lime at planting time and every winter after pruning. Neutralize highly alkaline soil by adding large quantities of milled pine bark to the soil and by on-going mulching with acid organics. Flower of sulphur can also be sprinkled around each plant every two to three months, especially if the water is also alkaline. Liberal additions of compost or other organic matter will improve any type of soil and will assist in neutralising the pH factor.

Seek advice from your local nurseryman who will most likely know the quality of the soil in the area. This could save you embarking on costly soil analysis.

PLANTING

In general, it is advisable to double-dig the whole rose bed or area, rather than making individual holes. Although roses have a shallow root system and are surface feeders, they need depth in the soil for anchoring and drainage.

1 Soak the area where you intend planting in advance, to make the soil more manageable.
2 Excavate the upper 30 to 40 cm of topsoil and place on side of bed.
3 Loosen subsoil to a depth of at least 30 cm by fork, pick or crowbar.
4 Add organics, e.g. compost, leaves, sawdust, peanut shells, and mix with the loosened subsoil. Ensure that water is able to drain further down. If not, install a drainpipe.
5 Liberally spread compost, milled pine bark and a little manure as well as a sprinkling of superphosphate and/or bone meal and a general fertilizer over the topsoil initially placed on the side of the bed.
Mix well.

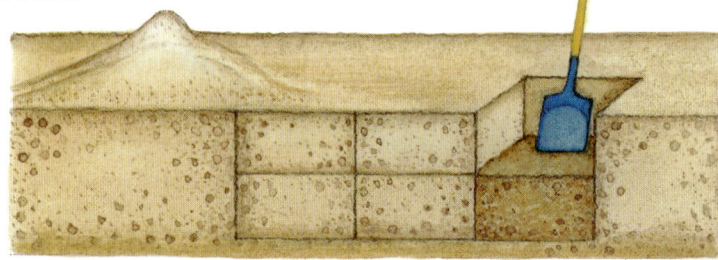

Excavate the upper 30 to 40 cm of topsoil and place it to one side of the bed; loosen the subsoil, and prepare it as in step 4 above. Return enriched topsoil to trench.

24 Planting procedure

6 Shovel the mixed, enriched topsoil back into the bed. Drench the prepared bed with water. After a few days, it will be ready for planting.

7 Stake out the position of the roses and make holes that are just big enough to take the containers.

8 For each plant, slit and remove the polythene plant bag. Check the condition of the roots, and if they appear to be tight on the outside, loosen the root ball by breaking it open so that the roots make good contact with the fresh soil. If the root ball appears fresh and loose, leave it undisturbed.

9 Place the plant in the hole, making sure it is the correct height by adding or taking away soil from under it. If the bud union is already below the surface of the soil in the container, cover the top of the container root ball with only a very thin layer of soil. If the bud union is visible above the soil level in the container, it must be settled deeper, 5 to 6 cm below the level of the bed.

10 Once the plant is positioned correctly, fill in the enriched soil around it and firm down well with the feet to eliminate air pockets.

11 Form a basin around the plant.

12 Apply approximately 20 litres of water.

13 Firm the soil down again the next day.

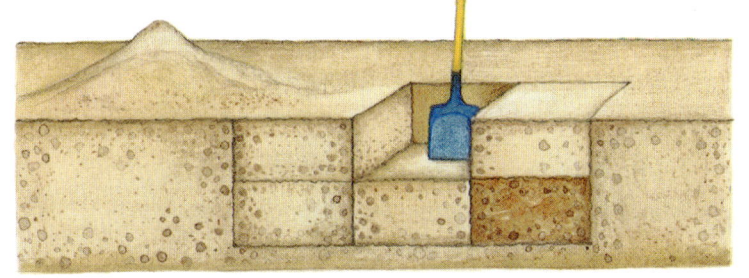

Repeat the routine with the second trench, and so on, until the entire bed – both topsoil and subsoil – has been loosened and enriched.

Ensure that the bud union is covered by a thin layer of soil.

Planting procedure 25

14 Once the soil has settled after two to three weeks, level the basin and mulch the bed.

15 Only in very stony or rocky gardens is it practical to prepare individual holes. In this case, dig holes 60 cm deep and 60 cm in diameter, taking out any large rocks. Add soil if necessary, plus four spades of compost, one spade of manure, one handful of garden fertiliser and one handful of bone meal or superphosphate. Mix this prior to planting. Fill the hole with water to soak the sub-soil and to ensure there is good drainage. Proceed with planting as described above.

When planting roses with bare roots, it is essential that no fertiliser, manure or fresh compost should touch the roots. Therefore, prepare holes or beds three to six months prior to planting. Alternatively, place a thin, protective layer of pure unmixed soil around the bare roots.

TRANSPLANTING OLDER ROSES

June is the best month of the year for transplanting roses. Roses are moved around the garden because of increased shade from nearby trees and shrubs; to give a general face lift to the garden; or when the roses have simply not performed over the past year or years. High rainfall can raise the groundwater level in the garden, and standing water at the root zone (between 30 and 50 cm down) is detrimental to the shrubs, necessitating their transplanting.

When planning to transplant roses, it is always best to prepare the new location first – follow the above procedure to prepare the bed. The same method applies when preparing individual holes, which should be at least 60 cm wide.

The rose bushes to be moved should be pruned or cut back considerably before they are dug up. This latter task is made easier if two people participate, with two spades.

A climbing rose can be planted at an angle next to a wall. This ensures adequate space for the roots, while enabling the rose to 'lean' against the wall for support.

Prepare the ground well in advance of planting bare-root roses, to ensure that fertilizers do not damage the roots.

The blade of the spade is pushed down repeatedly in a full circle about 20 cm from the centre of the bush, cutting any roots that spread beyond this area. Once the full circle has been achieved, the spades are simultaneously pushed down opposite one another and tilted, and the bush is lifted from the ground. If there is considerable resistance in lifting the bush, it means some major roots have not been cut. Rather than levering or pulling the bush too vigorously, use the spade to cut such roots cleanly before attempting again to lift the rose. When this is done, shake off the remaining soil and place the bush in a bucket of

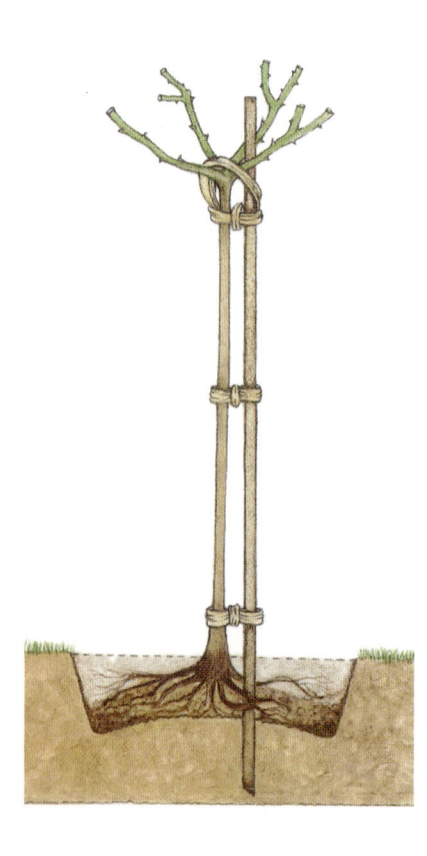

Use a strong stake to hold a Standard stem upright, and secure the stem with ties, taking particular care to secure the bud union at the top of the stem.

water, or keep it under moist hessian. Take special care not to leave the bush in the sun at all. Immediate replanting is ideal, but bare-root roses can safely be kept for several days in cool and moist conditions.

Before replanting, check the roots and remove those that are broken, as well as cutting away dead, woody parts at the crown or bud union. Be careful not to replant too deeply: the bud union should be just below the soil level. Water the newly planted roses well, using a hand-held hose in order to expel trapped air. Only weekly watering is required until mid-August when new growth is visible and temperatures have risen.

PROPAGATING ROSES

Propagating rose plants is more of a horticultural challenge than a cost saving. It is, of course, exciting to root cuttings, and even more so to succeed in bud-grafting a rose bush – but it does require dedication and 'green fingers'. Here are some tips on how to go about it.

Rooting cuttings

Although it is relatively easy to root hardwood cuttings of certain types of understock, such as Rosa multiflora 'Brooks '48' and hardy Climbers such as 'Cecile Brunner', most hybridized varieties present problems resulting from the softness of the wood and the high percentage of pith in the stems. It is considerably easier to root rose cuttings in colder regions, where rose stems go into dormancy in April and have time to mature and harden. Cuttings made in July and heeled into a sandy bed have several weeks to form a callus and take root, before rising temperatures force them to sprout. By contrast, rooting using the same method in warmer winter regions has a comparable success rate of only about 1%: hardwood cuttings made from the clippings of winter pruning, and laid into rooting pots or beds, will soon start to sprout, only to wilt a few weeks later, since no roots have been formed.

However, it is possible to get around this problem by simulating cold conditions. Take about 20 hardwood cuttings of between 10 and 15 cm, remove the thorns and wrap the cuttings lightly in water-absorbent tissue paper, moistened but not dripping wet. Place them in a clear plastic bag, without rooting hormone; seal the bag to avoid evaporation and store it in the fridge for a month or longer to allow the cuttings to form calluses on their wounds.

From a healthy bush, take a cutting about 20 cm long and the thickness of a pencil; cut off the soft tip and remove the thorns and lower leaves, with just one or two sets of leaves remaining. Dip in rooting hormone before planting in sandy soil.

Make a hole in the soil, and plant the cutting up to half its length.

Planting procedure 27

Now plant the individual cuttings to half their depth in small plant pots, in a porous mixture of sand, compost and peat moss or milled pine bark. Stand the pots in a shady position for a few weeks and keep just moist, but not over-watered. When leaves begin to sprout, move the pots into a more sunny position to 'harden off'; and when the new roses seem sufficiently strong, plant them out in a garden bed. Most 'own-root' rose plants do not grow as vigorously in their first year or two as do plants budded on rootstock. But once they are established, their performance is comparable.

A second method of propagating roses on their own roots is to make softwood cuttings. This is done just before the flower bud opens. Cut a stem off the bush, then cut it into pieces, leaving three leaves on each piece, and not using the very soft tip. Store these prepared cuttings for one night in a plastic bag in the fridge. Plant them next day, either in a rooting mist bed or in a tiny rooting greenhouse made from a 2-litre plastic cooldrink bottle. Cut the bottle horizontally in two, 8 cm from the bottom; punch drainage holes in the bottom, and fill up to 6 cm with coarse sand. Plant the cuttings in the sand and soak well with water. Slip the top part of the bottle over the bottom, making sure it is sealed. Keep such bottles on a south-facing windowsill. With screw caps closed, they should require only a little water once every two weeks.

Budding on an understock

Rose nurseries generally bud-graft roses on to understock (also known as rootstock). You therefore need to secure an understock plant, or find a source where the understock has grown out from a budded rose – especially easy to find on a Standard rose. Hardwood cuttings from long, smooth, thornless canes can be made in June/July, about 20 cm in length. To prevent sucker shoots emerging from below the bud union, it is advisable to carve out the lower eyes, but leave two or three at the tip. Plant the cuttings to half their depth in 5-litre plant bags or pots, or in a well-prepared garden bed, and spaced 20 cm apart. With normal watering, these cuttings should root and sprout, and be ready for budding by mid-October. By this time, the scion material or budwood of the chosen variety should also be ready for use. The budwood stem is mature when the petals start to scatter. Break off the thorns and remove the leaves. Budwood sticks can be kept for several days in the fridge, wrapped in moist paper or standing in a glass of water. You need a sharp knife for budding, and a 1-cm-broad strip of thin plastic from, say, a shopping bag for tying. Select a smooth area on the understock stem and slice the bark with a downward cut of the knife, leaving a lip at the bottom to hold the eye. Thinly slice the eye off the budwood stem and push the section below the eye between the sliced lip and stem of the understock. Now tie the eye securely in place using the plastic strip, and leave for about three weeks. If the eye has taken, it will start sprouting. To encourage sprouting, cut the top growth of the understock half way down; and if, after two months, the eye still looks fresh but has not sprouted, cut the understock stem off about 1 cm above the eye.

Roses are relatively shallow-rooted plants, and flourish in containers.

Budding on an understock

Anatomy of a Rose

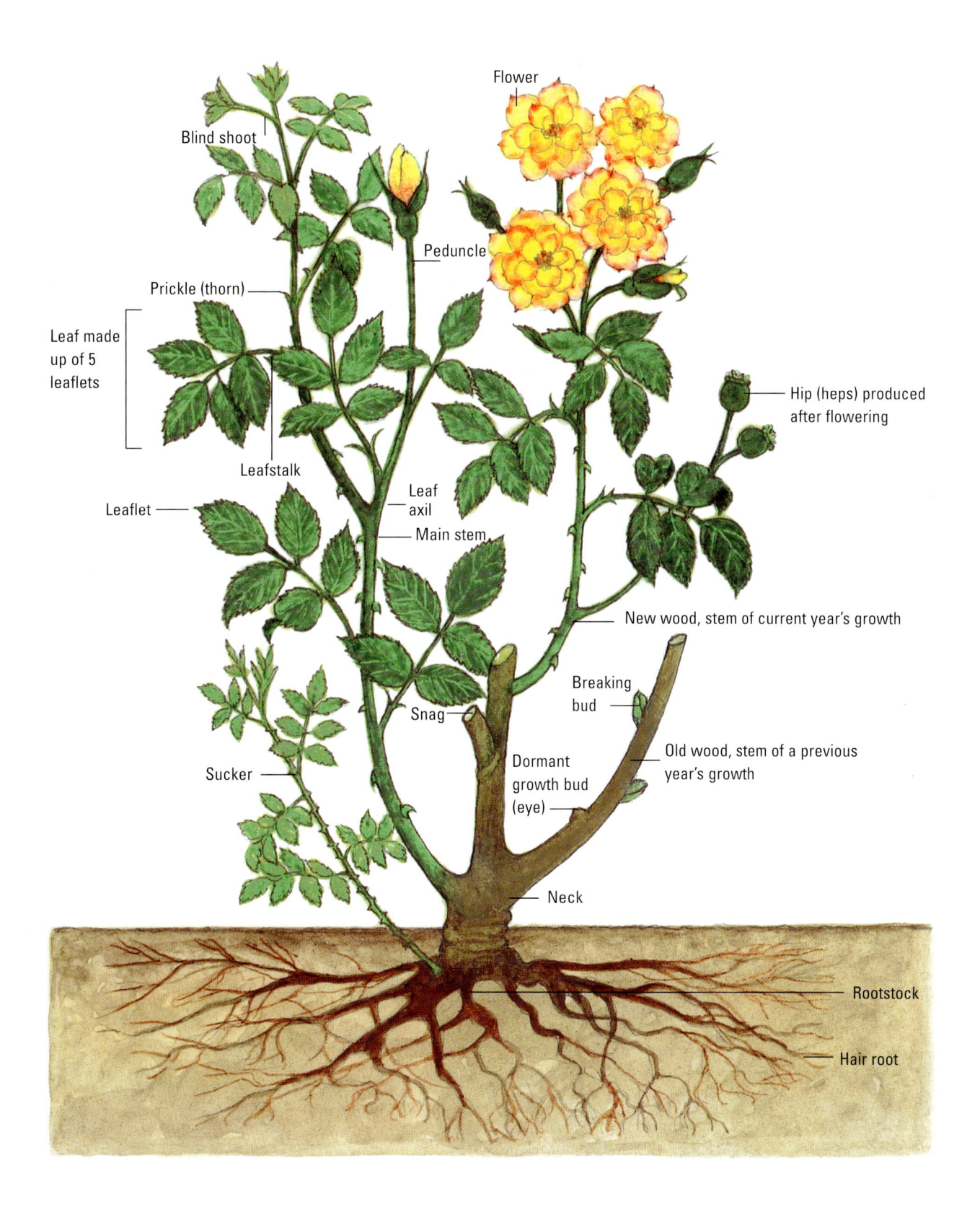

Rose care

Roses are particularly rewarding plants to grow – they respond quickly and gratifyingly to extra care. Once they are satisfactorily planted in a sunny position (and in the absence of disease), the health and performance of your roses will be determined by watering, fertilizing, grooming and pruning.

WATERING

Adequate water, ideally in combination with fertilizer, is important in determining the quality and extent of new growth. The quantity and intervals of watering depend not only on rainfall and on the soil type and thickness of the mulch, but also on temperature. You might decide to irrigate thoroughly once a week in moderate weather, and every day during very hot periods, to cool down the plants as well as to compensate for the loss of moisture from evaporation.

At all times, make sure that the irrigation period is sufficiently long for water to penetrate the mulch and soil and reach the roots. Unsatisfactory performance can often be attributed to lack of water, even when plants are watered every day. Water can be prevented from penetrating down to the roots if, for instance, there is too thick a layer of mulch; or if the plants are irrigated with too fine a spray and for too short a period for water to roll off the leaves and reach the roots. On slopes or embankments, it is essential to create a basin on the lower side of the plants in order to hold sufficient water to penetrate down to the roots.

The quality of the water can limit rose growing in some regions. When irrigation water contains relatively high proportions of sodium combinations, the absorption of some micronutrients, such as iron, is blocked and the leaves manifest a light-green to yellow appearance. If the sodium in the soil is not flushed out occasionally by rain water, the situation compounds and the roses deteriorate further and may die.

Overhead or subfoliage irrigation are both acceptable, although moisture from overhead irrigation can spoil open blooms. Watering should not take place late in the afternoon during autumn or on overcast days, as water standing on leaves for several hours can cause germination of black spot spores.

Rain is irrigation from heaven. It is nevertheless advisable to ensure that rain has indeed been sufficient to penetrate deeply, otherwise additional watering becomes necessary. An irrigation system is essential in a rose bed, if not for the whole garden. Garden centres offer advice on available options.

FERTILIZING

Regular fertilizing of roses during the growing season is essential, and plants react promptly to additional nutrition. However, fertilizer is not the solution to all ills – and two handfuls of fertilizer are not invariably better than one. Roses are often burned by having too much fertilizer placed in a heap next to the main stem or sprinkled in a narrow circle around it. Fertilizer is only of use when it is dissolved by water and carried to the roots, which are more or less confined to the space in the rose bed or hole in which they were planted.

Sprinkle a handful of Wonder Rose 8:1:5 (25) over each bush once a month or even every six weeks until about April. Very keen rosarians might prefer to fertilize lightly every week or every fortnight, in which case the handful is applied to three plants instead of one. Other combination fertilizers such as 2:3:2, 5:1:5, 3:2:1 and 3:1:5 are also suitable and so are the Guano-type fertilizers – in all cases, a handful (50 g) per rose bush, sprinkled over at least half a square metre, still applies. In cold regions, apply fertilizer only until the end of February or early March.

SUMMER IN THE ROSE GARDEN

Roses will have completed their second flowering cycle by early December. If a percentage of new shoots has been pinched, dead flowers picked fairly regularly, at least weekly, and blooms cut for display, flower production is more or less continuous. The term 'dead-heading' can be misleading, and might suggest the removal of only the dead flower head or hip, but this is quite wrong: the correct method is to cut back the stems of spent blooms about halfway down.

Light, early summer pruning

If regular grooming has not been carried out, early December is a good time to perform a light summer pruning. This entails cutting one 'tine' of forked stems; removing blind shoots and spindly inside growth; and undercutting stems that

Dead-heading

Disbudding

Rose care 31

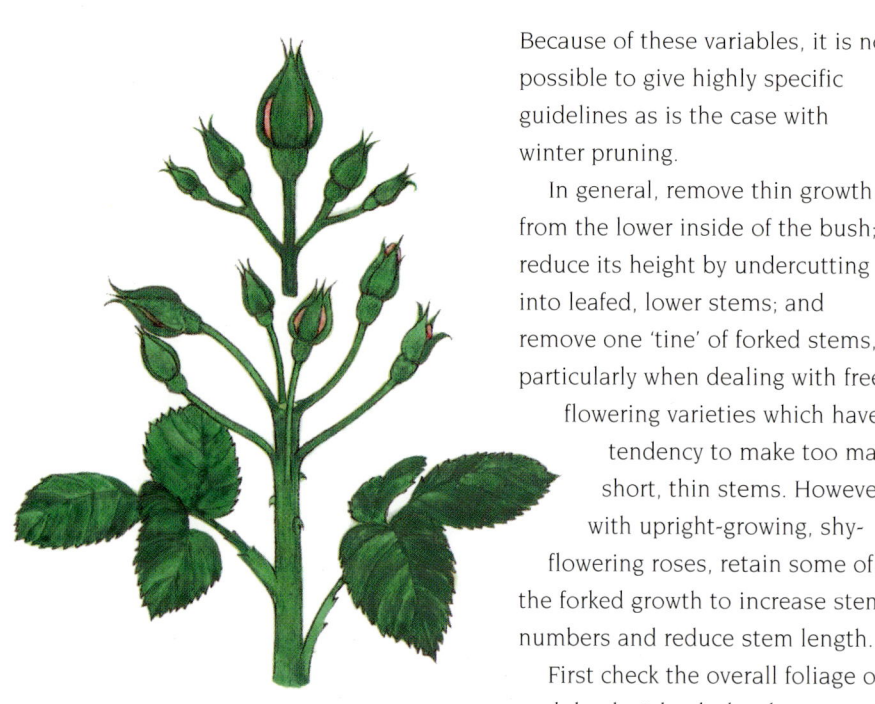

Removing centre buds to create a candelabra

are too tall, i.e. cutting halfway down the stem of the previous bloom, but only if what remains is in leaf and not denuded. It is important to cut back to just above a new shoot or an eye that has recently sprouted. This allows the new stem to grow that much stronger, producing a better bloom and encouraging new growth. By cutting back on to a new stem, the waiting period for new flowers is also much shorter. Any grooming in December makes pruning easier later on in the season.

Summer pruning

Summer pruning makes space for new growth and quality blooms and keeps the rose bush in a desirable shape. The best time for summer pruning is December/January.

The severity of summer pruning depends on how much pruning has been carried out between October and January, as well as on how much a bush has grown during this period.

Because of these variables, it is not possible to give highly specific guidelines as is the case with winter pruning.

In general, remove thin growth from the lower inside of the bush; reduce its height by undercutting into leafed, lower stems; and remove one 'tine' of forked stems, particularly when dealing with free-flowering varieties which have a tendency to make too many short, thin stems. However, with upright-growing, shy-flowering roses, retain some of the forked growth to increase stem numbers and reduce stem length.

First check the overall foliage on each bush. A bush that has grown too tall cannot be cut down to below existing foliage. If the rose blooms are now at an unreachable height and will be even more so with subsequent growth, the plant can only be cut back to the stage were there is still a good batch of leaves. If leaf growth starts only about 1 m from the base, for whatever reason, the bush can be reduced to about 1,3 m. If defoliation exists to an even higher point, it is advisable to remove only the thinner defoliated growth from the inside and all defoliated side stems, leaving all higher-up, leafed twigs and stems intact. The removal of defoliated growth is bound to result in strong new shoots sprouting at a lower level. Once these new shoots are mature, with green leaves, it is safe to cut back to just above such new stems.

Where bushes are leafy almost down to the base, summer pruning can be more severe, always considering that enough leaves must remain, but also enough top growth to shade the bare parts of the main stems at the base.

Miniature roses and Groundcover roses can be trimmed with hedge clippers. Again, be careful not to cut too low into defoliated wood. This is especially important when treating Groundcover roses. The lower shoots grow horizontally and are accustomed

Summer pruning – before and after

32 Rose care

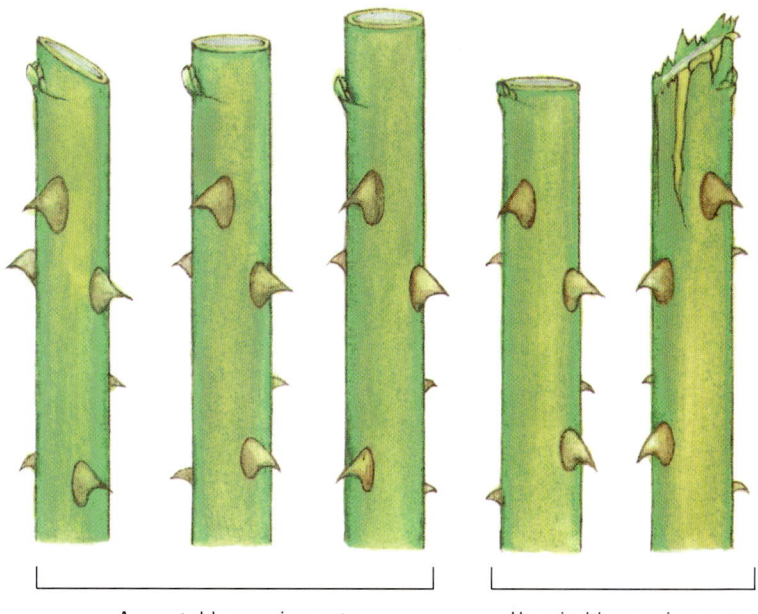

Acceptable pruning cuts   Unsuitable pruning cuts

to being shaded and protected by the upper growth. Sap flows much more slowly in horizontal stems than in vertical stems and, with this shade suddenly removed, the slow-flowing sap is heated up during a few hours of hot sun and the tissue can be killed below the bark. This can result in the dying back of such stems. The same occurs if weeds or leaves and branches of nearby plants and shrubs are allowed to shade all, or part of the roses, and this shade is suddenly removed. Rather carry out such tasks in stages or when a period of cool, rainy weather is anticipated.

It is advisable to spray with a double concentration of Dithane WG after summer pruning. The spray protects remaining leaves from fungus attack and the whitish residue reflects light and heat away from the bush for long enough until the sap flow in the plant is normalized and takes over the cooling function.

Rose growing is all about leaves. Whenever there is a sudden loss of leaves, be it from cutting too many blooms with too-long stems, from black spot or hail, the routine of the roots is disrupted. Hair roots die off and it takes one to two weeks before a new balance is established between leaf mass and root mass. Once this has taken place and you see new shoots appearing, it is time to fertilize.

Hail damage

Heavy hail with strong side winds can devastate rose bushes to such a degree that one has no option but to prune them drastically. With softer hail, damage becomes noticeable only a week or two thereafter. Wherever stems have been hit by hailstones, the bark starts splitting open and roses, unlike many other trees and shrubs, do not easily form a callus to seal such wounds. Fungal diseases can develop in the moisture and protection of the open wounds, and will spread from there to the leaves and newly formed shoots. To prevent diseases, spray the bushes thoroughly with a good fungicide, such as Dithane WG, Coppercount N, Bayleton, Mikal M or Copper oxychloride. In this instance, plants will not be harmed if two to three times the recommended strength is used.

Cut off any totally lacerated and broken stems as soon as possible after hail damage, retaining as many leaves as possible to help the bush recover more quickly. Once new shoots appear, especially from the lower part of the bush, and they have at least three new leaves, you can cut back the damaged growth more thoroughly. The leaves that were retained will have done their duty in keeping the roots stimulated. Badly damaged stems will never totally recover, so it is essential to rebuild the bush with basal stems, even if this only takes place with winter pruning. Wait until about two weeks after the hail to apply fertilizer.

Severe pruning

Rose care 33

WINTER PRUNING

Roses rejuvenate themselves by producing new stems from the base on a regular basis. Left unpruned, roses eventually carry out their own pruning by not nourishing the thinner inside growth, which slowly dries out completely and dies. In this case, new basal stems either push their way through the dead growth to flower higher up in the full light, or push up on the outsides of the bush or shrub, which becomes broader over the years.

We prune roses to maintain the shape of the bush, to keep the main branches to a manageable height, and to eliminate unsightly, superfluous dead wood. Pruning encourages strong new growth and reduces the number of flowering stems, resulting in an increase in eventual flower size.

Pruning shears

When to prune

Pruning should generally take place from mid-July until the end of August, with local weather patterns helping to pinpoint the time more exactly. For most parts of the country, the best time to prune is during the latter part of July. In warmer regions, such as the Lowveld and coastal KwaZulu-Natal, pruning can, if desired, be carried out by the end of June. Pruning is delayed in the very cold regions of the Eastern Free State, parts of KwaZulu-Natal close to the Drakensberg, as well as parts of the Karoo and Eastern Cape. It might vary from the first week in August in a climate such as Bethlehem to the last week in August in the really cold parts of the country. Bear in mind that pruning encourages sprouting even during fairly low temperatures. Newly sprouted leaves are tender and could be burnt by late frost, in which case nothing is gained and important stored reserves are lost.

In general, roses cannot be induced to flower earlier in spring by pruning early. However, delaying pruning by two to three weeks can result in a slight delay in flowering, possibly by up to a week.

Equipment

Pruning shears must be in good condition, as sharp blades make the job that much easier. Blades can be sharpened with a whetstone, available from hardware stores. Make sure to sharpen mainly the slanted outside of the blade and only very little on the flat inside. Continual sharpening of the inside will eventually create a gap between the blades. If there is play between the blades, tighten the centre nut gradually until the two blades are squeezed tightly next to one another. Before tightening the nut, allow a few drops of oil to penetrate between the two touching parts around the centre bolt and into the spring.

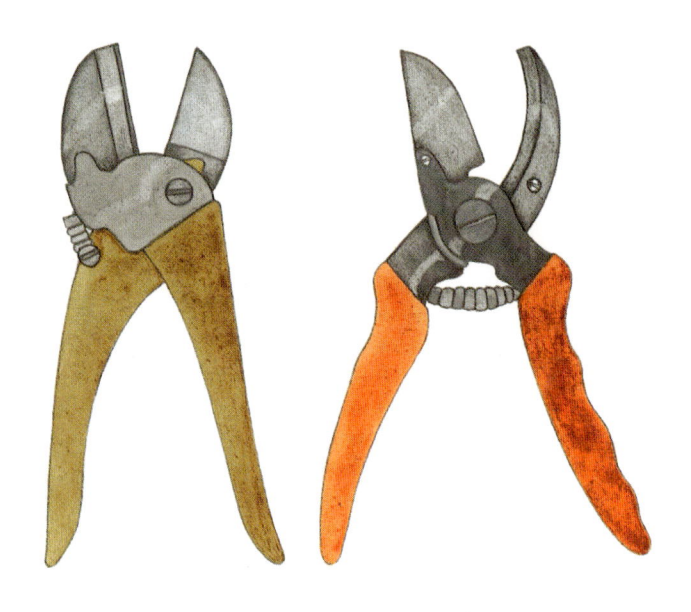

Using long-handled loppers of good quality, you can prune all types of roses without the assistance of a saw. The same principles of sharpening and of keeping the pivot bolt and nut tight apply to long-handled loppers.

Gloves, available from garden centres and hardware stores, make pruning more manageable, whether they're long-sleeved welding gloves or short gardening gloves.

How to prune

Bush roses (Hybrid Teas, Floribundas and the bush types of the English and Nostalgia roses)
For accuracy and neatness, make a pointed measure stick of about 1 m in length. Make a mark 10 cm from the point, which is the depth that it is to be pushed into the ground. Make a further mark 50 to 70 cm (according to personal preference) up from the first mark and cut off the stick at 20 cm above the second mark. Push this stick into the ground next to the bush to be pruned, and cut off every branch and stem in line with the top of the stick (70 to 90 cm above ground level). With the top growth and twigs removed, it becomes easy to inspect the bush and to select the main stems or branches that are to remain. The maximum number of stems or branches to

Before pruning

Bush rose prepruned to height of measuring pole

Pruned Bush rose – note that stems are cut at even height, corresponding to mark on measuring pole

remain is four and the minimum one. 'Branch' means a fairly thick wooden member that has branched more or less at the base and is two years or older. A 'stem' is this season's wooden growth from the base. The colour of the thorns helps distinguish between this season's stems and older wood. Thorns turn grey on old wood, but are usually still brown or reddish on this season's stems. The bark, too, is grey and thick on older wood.

First identify four suitable stems that are more or less neatly arranged in diverging directions. Remove all other stems and branches. If there are only one or two good stems, it is possible to retain some of the older branches. If the situation is not clear, start at the centre by removing older branches that are obviously in the way. However, if the branches do not look as if they could sustain new growth, cut away all older branches, retaining just one good stem, which should, ideally, be more or less in the centre. From this single good stem you can expect five to six good blooms, and alongside it, the development of new basal stems. Once you have selected the stems to remain, and removed all other stems and branches, check the measuring pole again, and cut the remaining stems at the mark that is 20 cm below the top. All remaining branches should be cut at the same height, give or take 10 cm, but not more. Remember that the root system will favour taller stems to the detriment of lower stems, a trend known as apical dominance.

The direction of the top eye is of minor importance – the rose will decide which eye to favour. The actual final cut should be at 90° to the stem. This is the smallest wound and since the stems are almost never absolutely vertical, it means that the cut is also not horizontal and will not collect water.

When cutting, make sure that the thick blade is facing up and is pointed away from you. If the thicker blade faces downwards it will bruise the stem severely. Another trick to make cutting easier is to grip the branch or stem well above where the cut is to be made, and to push gently away from the cutting blade of the shear. Very thick branches require vigorous pushing. Pushing stretches the wood and makes it softer to cut. If not familiar with this method, practise it higher up on the stems until you get the feel. If pushing is not synchronised with cutting, the branch might split. Pulling the stem backwards over the blade will make cutting almost impossible. The same technique applies to cutting very thick branches with loppers, where one can either use a foot or knee to push, or ask an assistant to help.

Rose care 35

Once the remaining stems have been pruned to the specified height, any side branches on these stems should be cut off smoothly next to the main stem. If any of the main stems is forked, remove one tine of the fork. Remaining stems should be separated from each other at the top by at least the length of the shears (about 20 cm).

Commence with the next bush. It gets easier all the time. However, no two rose bushes are identical, and adjustments have to be made. Where a bush is much weaker and shorter than the others, it is advisable to cut back such a bush more severely than the others. Much taller bushes are usually simply brought back to the standard 50 to 70 cm. They will grow as tall again, and as quickly.

Pruning a climber – step 1

Specimen Bush roses

The above method applies to Bush roses planted in beds, in groups and rows. Bush roses that are planted as single specimens or further apart than the recommended 50 to 80 cm, have more space to develop and can be pruned more lightly. This entails cutting them back to about 1 to 1,2 m. It still helps to remove growth, and particularly old wood, from the centre of the bush. Leave no more than four main branches, but allow substantial side stems on the main branches to remain, usually cut back to a length of about 20 cm. Such lightly pruned roses will produce quality blooms in October. Rose bushes that are pruned lightly every year form very thick wooden stems and remain bare – without foliage and flowers – at the lower part of the bush.

Spire roses

These are simply very tall Hybrid Teas, whose growth is formal and upright. They are planted for the purpose of screening or providing colour high up as a background. Prune Spire roses to chest height (1,3 m) and lop off all branches at this level. Then remove all surplus branches from the centre, again leaving not more than four main branches. When it comes to cleaning up the remaining main stems or branches, leave some of the stems on the upper level. Make sure that the tops of remaining stems are spaced about 30 cm from each other.

Bush rose pruning

Shrub roses

There are two ways of handling this group of roses. They can be pruned more or less like Spire roses, which will encourage strong new stems and large flowers in spring. However, if the graceful, arching habit of an informal shrub is required, do not cut off the shrub at a certain height but rather start by identifying the younger, better stems, and then removing older wood at the base. Since growth is usually very dense, it is advisable to pull out each main branch as it is cut, and then to re-check which other stems can be removed. Space must be created for new growth in the centre of the shrub. Cut back long, arching canes to where they start growing horizontally, as last season's hanging stems will not give rise to quality blooms. However, the weight of new growth and flowers will recreate the arching effect. Again, all or most of the shorter side stems are cut off smoothly next to the main stem.

Climbing roses

Some Climbing roses grow to such size and profusion that it becomes an impossible task to prune them. You can leave them unpruned, or

36 Rose care

simply tidy up at the base by cutting off obvious non-flower-bearing wood and stems. Since the bulk of the flowers are usually at such a height that one cannot see the detail of each bloom, the concern here is for profusion of blooms rather than individual quality.

However, if you feel that the rose has grown out of hand, pull up a ladder and reduce the growth drastically, always bearing in mind that cutting back such a strong rose will result in even more new growth and, usually, fewer flowers. It is best, before commencing pruning, to remove all ties holding the long branches in place. Cut away older branches in favour of new ones and then tie back the remaining branches on to the fence, pole, pergola etc. The most spectacular show can be achieved by tying long, climbing stems horizontally on to a fence or wall. Again, all side stems are cut off next to the main stems.

Another way of handling Climbers and also several of the large shrub and climbing types of English rose, is to bower the long canes and tie their tips at the base of the plant or on special pegs driven into the soil.

If a Climbing rose in your garden does not flower, try leaving it alone. Some Climbers need two years before they have done most of their growing and are ready to start flowering.

Pruning will encourage them to grow again, but not necessarily to flower. If this means that the rose is too large and unwieldy where you have planted it, and does not perform as you wish, take it out and transplant it to another, more appropriate spot, or give it to someone who has more space.

Pruning a climber – step 2

Fixing a climber to the wall

Tying the branches of an Umbrella Standard rose into a shape

Miniature roses

There are two pruning options here. One is to chop off all stems about 10 cm above soil level and then to cut out the ground shoots, leaving about four. If the Miniature is grown as a specimen and has achieved a substantial height and width – about 80 cm high and wide – use hedge clippers to trim it by a third or half. Older, woody stems can be removed from the centre. It is too time-consuming to prune the numerous little twigs. The rose will sort itself out and flower beautifully in spring. We do not expect large blooms from miniature roses, but rather an abundance of flowers.

Rose care 37

Groundcover roses
These grow into a dense, matted bush or low shrub. They can be left unpruned, but this might bring on red spiders early in the season. If weeds have become established amongst them, clip the roses well with hedge shears, and then remove some or all of the older wood, as well as the surrounding weeds.

'Iceberg'
This variety is exceptional in that it is able to flourish year after year on old wood without having to renew itself from the base. This is why 'Iceberg' is able to grow into quite a large shrub and to flower every day of the season. No other variety matches this ability.

Large shrubs of 'Iceberg' can be pruned lightly year after year and they will still produce the same quantity and quality of flowering clusters. However, if you wish your 'Iceberg' to remain a 'tame' bush that fits in with other Floribundas, prune in accordance with the instructions for Bush roses.

Standard roses
These are essentially Bush roses, and are pruned in almost the same way. However, do not use the measuring stick as described for Bush roses. Instead, cut back all stems and branches to about 50 cm of the crown or bud union and then remove all older wood and twigs. Final pruning should leave the stems about 30 cm long.

Miniature Standards are obviously cut even shorter unless they, too, are expected to perform as small shrubs.

Umbrella Standards are also tidied up by cutting off all the side stems and twigs and by shortening the arching canes.

Aftercare
Pruning stimulates root activity and sprouting of dormant eyes. The speed of development is partially dependent on temperature, but also on the water and nutrients available. It is obvious that watering and feeding should commence fairly soon after pruning has been completed.

1 Water the bed or soil around the rose bushes thoroughly, especially if watering has been applied sparingly over the past weeks during dormancy.
2 Check the soil condition in the rose bed by digging with a garden fork and getting a feel of the soil structure at root level. The soil should crumble in your hand. If it is hard and lumpy, air and water have difficulty penetrating down to the roots, resulting in poor root development. Poor soil condition is remedied by introducing organic material such as compost, old manure, peanut shells, and milled pine bark, even partially decomposed leaves and lawn clippings. Mix this material with the soil by digging it over to the depth of the fork tines. Try not to loosen strong roots: reposition the fork if it meets resistance from roots.

Be careful not to raise the soil level in a rose bed year after year by introducing compost and mulch. This can cause the root system eventually to be settled too deeply, where the soil remains too cold and wet for the

Pruning a Standard rose

Rose care

development of micro-organisms.

The roots of roses should be encouraged to grow downwards and to find the best level for developing a fine hair root system. This is the best time of year to help establish such growth habits. Digging out a plant that has performed poorly can show whether it has been too deeply covered. If so, there are two ways of addressing the problem. Either simply remove most of the composted top layer in the rose bed down to the correct level – where the bud union or knob is just covered with soil – and then loosen the topsoil, so that remaining compost can penetrate down to the deeper level where the main roots are embedded. If insufficient composted soil remains at this level, remove a further layer of about 10 cm, restore some of the compost, and proceed to dig it in. Alternatively, dig up the rose bush, cut away roots that have formed higher up and above the bud union and replant the rose after having dug over the bed and mixed the good topsoil with some of the subsoil.

It is a good idea to sterilise the soil in the rose bed at this time – provided you first remove all the roses. Drench the loose upper soil with a solution of one cup of Jeyes fluid in 10 to 15 litres of water, sprinkled over about 5 m^2. Two to three days later, water the area well again and after a few more days, dig it over. It is now ready for replanting. Another good soil sterilizer is Basamid, available from most garden centres. Sprinkle this powder over the bed and water in well. A week after application, dig the bed over, and after a further two to three days, it is ready for planting. The pruned, dug-up rose bushes can be heeled in or kept in buckets of water for a week and longer.

3 The first fertilizing of the season is carried out soon after pruning. If organics are also being dug into the soil, it is easier to spread both fertilizer and organics over the soil surface and to dig them in together. If, however, the existing mulch has decomposed and now consists of a thin layer of compost, spread just the fertilizer over the old mulch and mix together with the top 10 cm of soil. See page 30 for the recommended fertilizing procedure.

4 Water well again after having dug over the soil. Any loosened roots must be well embedded in the soil, and this can only be achieved with heavy watering.

5 Spray with lime sulphur or Oleum, although this is not essential if you have adhered to a regular spraying programme throughout the season. One part of lime sulphur is diluted with five parts of water. If pernicious scale is present on the lower parts of the stems, mix 100 ml of Oleum in 10 litres of water and add 10 ml of Metasystox or Ripcord for best results.

6 The rose or stalk borer seems to smell open cut wounds, and if they are in the vicinity they will drill down the soft pith found in the centre of a rose stem. If you have sprayed diligently with an insecticide during the season, the borer insect will likely have been eradicated from the garden. If not, it is best to seal all cuts with Steriseal, ordinary PVC paint or with a little clay.

Standard roses in containers give special emphasis to sunny spots.

7 Mulch keeps the soil cool and retains moisture, but a thick application early in the season when temperatures are still low actually prevents the soil from warming up. It is better to start a fresh layer of mulch towards the end of August.

8 From now on, water the rose bed weekly, increasing to twice weekly once the roses show rapid growth and temperatures have increased. Spraying of roses is usually only necessary by the end of September, when powdery mildew could start curling the new leaves and when the American bollworm starts to lay eggs on the green buds. Thrips will also start being active in the soft tissue of the roses long before damage is evident on the petals. It is therefore advisable to start spraying with an insecticide and spreader in mid-September – before problems manifest themselves.

Rose care

Pest and disease control

Spraying roses for the control of pests and diseases must be carried out thoroughly and with a good understanding of both pest and remedy. Pesticides are chemical compounds that control insects and diseases on plants, and comprise insecticides, fungicides and acaricides (for the control of red spider). To be effective, it is crucial that the stems, leaves and blooms should be totally covered with the spray solution, and that it must run behind dormant eyes where spores and eggs of red spiders and thrips are harboured.

Roses should be sprayed regularly, at least fortnightly; and in rainy, humid weather conditions, virtually on a weekly basis. There are a few exceptions to this rule: mainly roses that are unusually disease-resistant – particularly Groundcover roses or large Climbers such as 'Mermaid'.

By adhering to a good spraying programme, it is possible to enjoy successful rose growing even in the hot, humid climate of Durban and its surroundings, as well as in the cool, moist spring and autumn weather of the Eastern and Western Cape. In the very dry, semi-desert regions of the Karoo and Kalahari, red spider (more accurately the two-spotted spider mite) presents a serious problem. In summer rainfall regions, it is important to spray during the rainy summer and moist, cool autumn, rather than in the dry, hot spring.

It makes sense to control a range of different pests and diseases with one application, by combining pesticides in a 'cocktail'. Pests and diseases become resistant to specific chemicals if these are used continuously, so it is good practice to alternate pesticide cocktails.

The following information should help you identify diseases and be aware of the seasons during which they are specifically prevalent. This will enable you to mix the correct cocktail. Wherever specific product brands are mentioned for treating problems, remember that any other brands containing the appropriate active ingredients are also suitable.

Powdery mildew

FUNGAL DISEASES
Powdery mildew

This fungus starts developing on the soft, immature leaves of the new growth often before the formation of the flower bud. It is noticeable at first by a slight curling of the leaves and light discolouration on their undersides. Next, a white powder appears and spreads quickly, preventing leaves and flower buds from developing. Certain varieties are particularly susceptible to this fungus, and gardeners who are not keen on spraying should avoid these varieties.

To control powdery mildew: Rosecare, which also has a limited effect on black spot and aphids; Bayleton A, an excellent, multipurpose fungicide controlling powdery mildew, black spot and downy mildew; sodium bicarbonate, together

Pest and disease control

Powdery Mildew

with a mineral oil such as Oleum or Citrex – a curative and preventative spray (use late in the afternoon and never during the heat of the day); Funginex controls powdery mildew and black spot.

Black spot
This is a fungus that germinates mostly on the lower, mature leaves of roses and requires several hours of actual wetness before it enters the leaves. Several days later, one or more serrated black spots appear on the leaf, causing it to yellow, and eventually to drop off. Black spot appears mainly during rainy periods and when heavy dew occurs. During such periods you need to spray weekly, and even more often if there are heavy downpours that wash spray off the leaves.

To control black spot: Dithane WG, containing mancozeb, is very effective in preventing black spot and downy mildew; Coppercount-N (copper suspended in a liquid solution, and also containing some ammonium); Sporgon, a prochlaraz manganese chloride complex known as imidazole, is the only chemical that actually stops black spot from further development.

Black spot   Downy mildew

Downy mildew
Recognized for centuries as a grape disease, downy mildew has only recently (in the last 15 years) evolved a strain that is harmful to roses. It is a fungus that develops on the upper leaves and is identified by irregular black-brown patches. It not only causes leaves to drop, but affects stems as well, and blocks and destroys the capillaries in the peduncle, arresting flower development. Downy mildew develops only in moist, misty and cool conditions, but will not germinate when the temperature rises above 18°C.

To control downy mildew: Dithane M45 or WG and Bayleton are effective against the spread of downy mildew, as are Mikal M and Ridomil. Previcure N keeps the affected capillaries open until the disease is controlled either by application of a pesticide or by a change in the weather.

Pest and disease control

Rose rust
Another fungal disease that develops mainly during cool and moist weather conditions. It is identified by orange pustules on the undersides of the leaves, which later become powdery. Some varieties are much more susceptible to this than others.
To control rose rust: apply Plantvax.
All the above-mentioned fungicides are nontoxic, in the sense that they will not kill insects nor are they harmful to pets if used in the correct dosage.

HARMFUL INSECTS, BEETLES AND MITES
Insects and pests can also be detrimental to the development of leaves and flowers. Most available insecticides are effective against most of the insects listed below. A suitable insecticide is part of the recommended cocktail. However, if you are unwilling to use insecticides in your garden, leave them out of the cocktail and spray for fungal diseases only. Where possible, alternative methods are suggested for controlling insects, beetles or mites.

American bollworm
The American bollworm burrows through the tight flower bud, resulting in punctured petals when the bloom opens, and sometimes with the centre of the bud chewed. The moths fly at night and lay their eggs on the sepals of immature buds. Spray the buds with an insecticide such as Ripcord or Karbasol to prevent further development of the eggs, and to prevent the worms from hatching. The eggs are clearly visible on the buds and can also be rubbed off or squashed.

Aphids or greenfly
Aphids or greenfly are tiny insects that appear very suddenly on the juicy tips of young rose shoots, usually in early spring and late autumn. Even without being sprayed, aphids usually disappear as the stems mature and can no longer be punctured so easily. To treat just a few rose plants, use the aerosol formulation of pirimikarb, namely Pirimor or Garden Gun. Metasystox, Garden Ripcord, Karbasol and Malasol are other effective insecticides.

Chafer
The chafer, Christmas or peanut beetle is nocturnal and chews the leaves until they look like lace. Ripcord or Karbasol sprayed on the leaves kills chafers. An efficient, non-chemical method of controlling these beetles is to set up a light trap at night: hang an illuminated light bulb near the roses. Directly beneath the light source, place a bucket of water, on which a thin layer of oil has been poured. Beetles are attracted by the light and will crash into the bulb, and then drop straight down into the bucket.

Fruit chafers
Fruit chafers and CMR beetles are attracted by rose scent, and chew the flowers. A simple trap can be made using an empty, two-litre, plastic cooldrink bottle. Cut three or four two-cm-wide holes about halfway up the sides. Make a few small holes at the bottom to allow for rainwater drainage. Peel and slice a banana and place it in the bottle. Tie the trap on a tall stake above the rose flowers. Beetles collect in the bottle, and must be removed regularly – they can be thrown in a bucket half filled with water and a little oil. Refresh the banana when necessary to keep a fresh scent in the bottle.

Pernicious scale
Pernicious scale settles on the main stems at the base of the rose and then multiplies, moving up the stems and even settling on the leaves. The insect is protected by its shell and not easily killed. It is best controlled in winter after pruning, when only a few stems remain: the scale can be brushed off with a solution of lime sulphur or Oleum. The presence of scale is a sure indication that the root system of the rose is unable to develop freely, either because of soil compaction, poor drainage or, if the rose is in a container, because it has become root-bound. Once the cause has been identified, it can be rectified.

Pest and disease control

Red spider

Red spider, also known as the two-spotted spider mite, is a dreaded pest. They are most devastating during drought conditions and whenever the moisture content of the leaves is insufficient. Once they have started breeding, it is difficult to control their development. They lay eggs on the undersides of the lower leaves. Mites hatch after a few days and are able to lay their own eggs almost immediately. They protect themselves by spinning an invisible spider web. The spider mites suck chlorophyll out of the leaves, giving them a mottled effect and eventually causing leaf drop. Control by insecticide is difficult, since they are able to build up resistance to a poison after repeated applications. An old and effective way of preventing them from breeding is by hosing the plants from the underside upwards once or twice a week. Apollo is effective and nontoxic – it hardens the skin of the eggs and larvae, preventing them from hatching. It must be sprayed very thoroughly, three times, at five-day intervals, to ensure that all newly laid eggs as well as mature mites have been eliminated. Rape Oil Insecticide, an organic oil that is water 'mixable', is nontoxic and acts by suffocating the mites. As when treating with all other acaricides, it is essential that the undersides of the leaves should be thoroughly wetted when spraying. Spidermite-cide kills all spider mites, eggs and larvae with two applications, administered one week apart.

Rose borer

The rose borer is generally not regarded as a harmful insect. It burrows or drills through the soft pith down the centre of the stem, where it lays eggs and then catches flies as food for the hatching larvae. Roses can still grow with partially hollowed stems, and strong plants are not affected by it. Weaker bushes tend to develop dieback from such hollowed canes. Regular spraying with an insecticide for thrips and other insects should also take care of the rose borer.

Thrips

Thrips are tiny insects that settle between the petals of tight buds and start rasping the petals' edges. These insects can be devastating and, once they have become established, can destroy every bloom on the plant. The breeding cycle stretches from eggs that develop in the soil, through two larval stages on the leaves, to the mature insect in the flower. They are able to fly and are also carried by the wind. Other plants and weeds may act as host plants. To control thrips, it is essential to add an insecticide to every spray cocktail, and to spray thoroughly in order to make good contact with the larvae or insect. The smell of garlic is a deterrent to thrips, so it helps to add garlic powder to the cocktail.

Whitefly

Whitefly is not very prevalent on roses. If roses are targeted, it is because more accustomed host plants such as vegetables, fuchsias or violets are in the vicinity. Whitefly is easily controlled with insecticide.

PREPARATION OF COCKTAILS

Select ingredients for two or three of the cocktails given below, according to any diseases either noted on your roses or that you should anticipate in your particular climatic conditions. Weather patterns determine the correct choice of cocktail. For instance, during warm, dry periods, powdery mildew is prevalent, while black spot and downy mildew occur during long rainy spells, with high humidity and low temperatures at night. Try to alternate with at least two different cocktails, in order to avoid build-up of immunity by pests or diseases, and to allow for changing weather patterns.

In order to make pesticides more effective, it is essential to add to the cocktail either a 'spreader' or a 'sticker'. A spreader ensures an even spread on the waxy leaf surface of a film of water. G49 is a spreader, although it can be replaced with liquid soap. A sticker has a sticking action that ensures the fungicide stays on the leaves after the water has evaporated. This is especially important during regular spells of rain. Nufilm is a sticker, and this can be replaced with SprayStay or Wash 'n Wax.

You can add a suitable 'foliar food' to the cocktail, although experience has shown that this is of minor importance, with the exception of roses growing in compacted soil.

Pest and disease control 43

QUANTITIES

Approximately one litre of spray solution is needed for every ten rose bushes. This means that for 100 rose bushes, the minimum quantity of solution could be accommodated by a spray pump with an eight-litre tank. For more roses it is advisable to obtain a 15- to 20-litre knapsack spray. Note that 5 ml OR 5 grams is the equivalent of 1 level teaspoon; 10 ml OR 10 grams is the equivalent of a tablespoon.

The quantities stated for the cocktails below are for dilution in 10 litres of water. It is best, initially, to place the required ingredients in a one- or two-litre plastic container and mix well before pouring the mixture into the spray tank, which has already been filled or half filled with water. Shake the spray pump well before spraying.

These cocktails should never be premixed and stored, not for a week or even a day. Once the chemicals are mixed with water, their stability changes quickly and they will not be active for more than a few hours.

COCKTAIL RECIPES

Rosecare, a well-known product, has the same active ingredient as Funginex, and is recommended for use when just a few roses are grown. The Bayer broad-spectrum fungicide, Folicure, may be used as an alternative to Funginex in Cocktail 1 if the problem with powdery mildew persists.

Spider mites can only be controlled by spraying thoroughly on the undersides of the lower leaves. To save costs, it is often best to treat this problem separately.

• HOME-MADE COCKTAIL RECIPES •

Cocktail 1
15 ml Funginex, 10 ml Ripcord, 2,5 ml G49, 10 ml vinegar (for powdery mildew, light infection of black spot, aphids, bollworm, stem borer, thrips and beetles)

Cocktail 2
20 ml Citrex or Oleum, 10 g sodium bicarbonate, 10 ml Metasystox, 5 ml liquid soap, 10 g garlic powder (for powdery mildew, aphids, bollworm, stem borer, thrips)

Cocktail 3
20 g Dithane WG, 2,5 ml Nufilm N, 10 ml Ripcord (for black spot, downy mildew, aphids, boll-worm, beetles, thrips, stem borer)

Cocktail 4
25 g Bayleton A, 2,5 ml Nufilm, 10 ml Metasystox (for black spot, powdery mildew, downy mildew, aphids, bollworm, stem borer)

Cocktail 5
10 g Sporgon and 20 ml Coppercount (for black spot)

Cocktail 6
7,5 ml Previcure and 20 g Ridomil (for downy mildew)

• SPIDER MITE COCKTAILS •

Cocktail 1
2 tablets Talstar, 7 ml Apollo, 2,5 ml G49, 10 ml vinegar

Cocktail 2
30 ml Spidermitecide, 2,5 ml G49, (do not mix with any other pesticide)

Cocktail 3
100 ml Rape Oil Insecticide, 2,5 ml G49

Cocktail 4
1 cup of sugar boiled in 5 litres water (This should be used no more than twice in quick succession since, in the process of suffocating spider mites, it interferes with the evaporation process of the leaves.)

Queen Elizabeth

44 Pest and disease control

DEFICIENCY DISEASES

Rose leaves inform the observant gardener of the plant's wellbeing or of its problems. Large, deep green leaves indicate an active root system, well aerated, with enough moving water and adequate nutrients available for absorption. Stem length and flower size can be expected to be superlative. Smaller leaves can indicate heat stress and insufficient water, while discolouration of the leaves shows a deficiency of nutrients – see section on fertilizing, page 30.

Nitrogen deficiency

Nitrogen deficiency is indicated by pale green-yellow leaves and shoots. On an average rose bush, approximately 20 to 30 actively growing shoots extend, in total, by about 5 cm per day. This growth requires a considerable amount of nitrogen. Being water soluble, nitrogen is leached out of the soil more quickly than any other nutrient, particularly in sandy soil.

Iron deficiency

The most common deficiency is that of iron, where leaf veins remain green, but the areas in between gradually turn light green to yellow, and almost white in severe cases. An iron deficiency does not necessarily mean that there is no iron in the soil, but rather that it cannot be absorbed by the roots – usually the result of insufficient aeration due to soil compaction, over-watering or waterlogging. Without a good supply of oxygen in the root zone, micro-organisms are inactive and do not convert iron, manganese, boron, copper, sulphur and other essential trace elements into a form that can be absorbed by the roots.

Sudden loss of leaves (leaf drop caused by disease, removal of too many active leaves when cutting long-stemmed blooms, or hail) disturbs the balanced flow of sap, leaving the roots unable to absorb and transport trace elements. Signs of deficiency become apparent in the leaves within days.

When the soil contains relatively high percentages of lime or sodium (natrium combinations), causing high alkalinity, absorption of some micro-nutrients, including iron, is blocked. Acid organic material such as peat moss and milled pine bark helps regulate this problem, together with a handful of flower of sulphur sprinkled around each plant once or twice a year. (The condition will compound if caused by alkaline irrigation water.)

To rectify deficiencies

Ensure adequate aeration of the soil, and treat plants with trace elements in chelate form (for easy absorption by the leaves and roots), or add them to the spray cocktail. The most popular commercial product is Phostrogen, which contains all required nutrients. To correct deficiencies almost immediately, wet the leaves and drench the soil with 50 g of Phostrogen in 10 litres of water for about ten medium-sized bushes.

A common practice is the annual application of a tablespoon of Epsom salts (magnesium sulphate). Magnesium is an important trace element, responsible for the formation of chlorophyll, and is beneficial in alkaline soil where sulphate helps acidify the soil. In good, friable soil and normal conditions, this treatment, while not harmful, is not necessary.

Lack of nitrogen

Lack of iron

Lack of magnesium

Lack of phosphorus

Lack of potassium

Pest and disease control

PROBLEMS ARISING FROM EXTREME WEATHER CONDITIONS

Sunburn

Although sunburn is not a disease in itself, it does cause a secondary disease known as stem canker or coniothirium. This is caused by bacteria and no remedial sprays are available. It causes 'dieback' of part of the rose bush, or even the entire bush. A secondary fungus and bacteria settle in dead tissue almost immediately, and soon attack the surrounding healthy tissue as well. Black to purplish blotches become visible on the stem. The capillaries through which sap is transported are blocked or severed at this point and, once the dead tissue has encircled the stem, the above section shrivels and dies.

Sunburn occurs on the lower parts of the stems, usually on the curvature just above soil level. It can happen in early August, when the stems are still bare after pruning, and the sun rapidly warms frozen tissue after a frosty night. In regions that expect late frost, it is advisable to spray after pruning with a solution of 1 part lime sulphur to 5 parts water, or use limewash. The residual whiteness reflects sunlight.

Sunburn occurs more often and with more devastating results in the heat of summer, when the lower parts of the plant are not shaded by a canopy of leaves and when water in the surrounding soil is allowed to heat up because of insufficient mulch or cover. Sudden leaf drop (caused by black spot, spider mites, hail etc.) can slow down the sap flow so much that normal cooling processes – liquid moving through the capillaries – does not take place.

If blotches are apparent but have not spread too much, it is still possible to retain the affected stems by sealing them with Steriseal. The stems will put on new growth and, with the sap flow restored, callus growth around the edges of the infected areas will prevent the disease from spreading. Such branches can be removed at a later stage during routine pruning, by which stage new basal stems will have taken over.

Stem canker

Cold snap

A cold snap in September can burn the tips of soft, new shoots. This happens almost annually in the coldest regions of the country. If the cold is not too severe, it may turn out to be beneficial – by performing a good pinching of shoots, after which rose bushes will sprout very quickly again, and with renewed vigour. However, if the frost is very severe, symptoms of sunburn (described above) may occur.

Climatic conditions and weather patterns play a major role in determining the wellbeing of roses. Pre-emptive spraying can lessen the impact of adverse weather conditions.

Growing roses in containers

With good care, roses are able to flourish in pots and containers. A distinct advantage of container growing is that pots can be moved to ensure the standard requirement of at least five hours of sunlight daily – especially with the changing seasons.

It is important to select a size of container that matches the anticipated size of the rose one wishes to grow – water-holding capacity is central to success. In principle, a pot that holds 10 litres of water would suffice for a Miniature rose; a Bush Rose needs a water-holding capacity of at least 20 litres; and a large Climber needs a tub or drum with a capacity of at least 50 litres. On the other hand, three and even more roses can be planted in one large container, as long as each bush still has a soil volume of 20 litres.

The material out of which the container is made is of minor importance. It may be plastic, asbestos, concrete, wood or metal. Plastic is not as robust, and metal is likely to rust within a few years.

Container roses are expected to be feature plants, so it is advisable to select showy varieties that are vigorous, free-flowering and that develop a good plant shape. A tall-growing rose looks better in a tall container, and a bushy variety in a more compact container.

It is essential that the container has good drainage holes at the bottom or at the lowest point on the sides. With holes at the bottom, the container should stand on bricks or similar supports, not on soil or lawn, which could block drainage holes. The practice of placing pebbles, potshards, stones or similar material at the bottom is advisable, since it ensures long-term drainage.

The soil used should offer good drainage on the one hand, and water-holding capacity on the other. Ordinary potting soil is not good enough, since it will settle and compact after a year or two. A good mix is: one part garden soil; one part potting soil; one part pine bark mulch; one part pine bark chunks, or pecan nut shells or similar material; one part gravel or clinker ash; one part coarse river sand; and one part peat moss or peanut shells.

To every 20-litre volume, add one handful of bone meal, one handful of superphosphate and one handful of Wonder Rose (8:1:5) and mix in well. Moisten this growing medium before placing it in the container(s). Water the growing medium again in the container, and let it stand and settle for a day or two. Plant the rose, making sure that the bud union is just below the rim of the container, and not settled too deeply. Water the plant thoroughly.

Watering is now the key to success. During the first two months, water only every second or third day. After this period, the roots of the rose will have spread in the container, and it is now important to water every day. Water must be sufficient just to reach the bottom drainage holes. With less water, the lower parts will dry out, the peripheral roots will shrivel, and the rose will soon be riddled with spider mite – and could eventually die. Watering can be reduced during winter to twice a week, but the rose should never be allowed to dry out. Ground-cover plants look attractive planted round the edge of the tub; and pebbles or bark chips make good mulch.

Spread a tablespoon of Wonder Rose (8:1:5) every two to three weeks per every 20-litre volume. Fertilizer tablets are now available, and tests have shown that two AgrEvo Plant Fertilizer Tablets suffice for a 20-litre volume pot for six months.

Normal pest and disease control applies. However, in the more controlled environment of a container, it has been found that granular insecticide spread around the rose takes care of insects for about three weeks to a month.

Cut flowers

Ensuring a supply of rose blooms for home decoration is often a major incentive to gardeners to plant roses. Any of the various groups of roses can supply cut flowers, but the queen of cut flowers is the Hybrid Tea, which guarantees classical, long-stems.

It is important not to cut too many long-stemmed blooms in too short a period of time – the excessive loss of leaves and stems can disturb the sap flow and cause stress to the root system. A good principle is to cut the leading upper bloom approximately halfway down the branch, preferably above the fifth leaf. The bloom next to it is often the second tine of the fork and can be cut off at the point of branching. If the bush has many active, new shoots, the issue of leaving enough leaves behind is less important.

Blooms can be picked at any time of the day or night. Have a container half filled with water close by; place blooms in it within a few minutes of picking. From the moment the cut is made, air instead of water is sucked into the stem. Trapped air in stems and leaves causes wilting even after the flower is placed in water. When enough blooms have been picked, top up the container with water, place it in a dark, cool position and leave it to stand for a few hours. During this time, all systems 'shut down', with a minimum of evaporation taking place. When saturated from standing in the bucket, the blooms are ready for arranging. If blooms are kept out of water at this stage for a short period, even for an hour, they are able to stay fresh, since evaporation is now minimal.

Roses that have wilted prior to arranging (especially those bought at a supermarket or from street vendors) should be placed – or can simply be arranged – in hot water (about 40°C). Hot water contains less air than cold water and, as it is absorbed through the cut stem, it drives out any trapped air. Bubbles escaping from the cut are visible in a glass vase.

For an extended vase life, add 3 tablespoons of sugar and 1 tablespoon of vinegar or 1 teaspoon of Jik to about 1 litre of water. Sugar dissolves well in hot water and strengthens the petals and, to a limited extent, serves as a plant food. Vinegar or Jik prevents formation of algae, making it unnecessary to replace the water every day.

The stage at which the bud or bloom is picked depends both on the variety and on personal preference. One soon learns that varieties such as 'Johannesburg Sun', 'Monika', 'Summer Lady' and 'Cora Marie' open their long, slender buds relatively quickly and should be cut when the sepals are just starting to unfold. Large, full varieties such as 'Just Joey', 'Double Delight', 'Oklahoma' and 'Yankee Doodle' should be cut as half-open blooms, or at least when the outer petals have fully unfolded.

While taking care not to cut too many blooms from one bush, it is still essential to remove old flowers to stimulate the sprouting of new growth. Cut back stems about half-way – about 30 cm for a short-stemmed variety such as 'Electron'; and for the long-stemmed 'Andrea Stelzer', about 50 and even 60 cm. At least five leaves should remain on the stub. Cut away one tine of forked stems to channel the sap to a single point. It is not necessary to seal stems after cutting blooms.

The more often 'dead-heading' and grooming is carried out, the sooner new growth is stimulated and a never-ending supply of blooms can be expected. This does not apply to the same degree to Floribunda roses, which form clusters, and it often takes three weeks or more before all the buds in a cluster have opened. During this period, the bush starts to sprout new stems just below the cluster. When grooming, remove the whole cluster of spent flowers just above such new shoots. Miniatures and Groundcover roses are such busy plants that they require no more than occasional trimming.

Month-by-month guide to

MONTH	GROOMING	WATERING	FEEDING	SPRAYING
JULY	Perform severe winter pruning between middle and end of the month in all temperate climatic regions. Attend pruning demonstrations – there is always something new to learn.	Drench beds thoroughly after pruning. Keep on watering once every fortnight.	Spread a layer of about 5 cm of compost and/or manure on rose beds and around specimen plants. Sprinkle one handful each of fertilizer and Superphosphate around each bush and dig in to a depth of 20 cm.	Completely cover all stems and cuts with solution of one part lime sulphur to five parts water. Use Oleum (100 ml in 10 litres) plus Metasystox if pernicious scale is apparent.
AUGUST	Severe winter pruning in the coldest regions.	Increase watering to weekly applications, with a minimum of 20 mm sprinkled water or 10 litres per bush per week.	With increasing temperatures, bare soil in rose beds needs insulating with mulch or a cover of slates, bricks etc.	Control any infestation by greenfly of lush new shoots with a suitable insecticide.
SEPTEMBER	By mid-month, top off all deformed shoots or those growing in undesired directions and pinch about 30% of the tips of shoots. Disbud (break away) all side buds on Hybrid Tea roses to strengthen the terminal bud. Remove the terminal bud from clusters of Floribunda roses to ensure an even head of flowers. Check stakes and ties on Standard roses and renew if not in good order.	Watering is increased to twice weekly or to daily application of lesser quantity.	Towards end of month, start monthly fertilizing program. A small handful or 30 grams of Wonder Rose or similar product is sprinkled over each bush. Twice as much for climbers, less for very young and small bushes.	Start spraying by mid-September with the recommended cocktail 1 and alternate a week or fortnight later with cocktail 2. On the Cape coast, use cocktails 3 and 4. Check lower leaves for red spider and spray with one of the recommended spider mite cocktails.
OCTOBER	Disbud all newly appearing side buds. Top shoots that are unlikely to produce good blooms. Pick blooms for the house and cut the stems of dead flowers back to above the 5th leaf. Top basal shoots at knee height.	Adhere to the watering regimen of twice weekly, every second day or daily, according to irrigation system and availability of water and time. Each rose should receive a minimum of 10 litres per week.	Fertilize at end of month as per September. Remember that fertilizer is only activated when dissolved by water and carried to the roots. Do not sprinkle fertilizer over wet leaves. Brush off any fertilizer dust from foliage.	Adhere to the spraying programme. If the rainy season has started, alternate with cocktails 1 and 3.
NOVEMBER	Continue disbudding and dead-heading. Groom plants, cutting out weedy, thin shoots. Cut flowers for the home.	Follow your watering routine unless it rains.	Fertilize at end of month as per September. Mulch needs to be checked and replenished if it is not providing sufficient heat insulation.	Carry on spraying alternately with cocktails 1 and 3 every fortnight. If powdery mildew is a problem, spray weekly, alternating between cocktails 1, 2 and 3.

successful rose growing

MONTH	GROOMING	WATERING	FEEDING	SPRAYING
DECEMBER	If absent from home for an extended period, attend to cutting and grooming after your return. To enjoy good roses over the festive season, carry on with dead-heading, disbudding and grooming.	Follow your watering routine unless it rains.	Fertilize at end of month as per September.	Carry on spraying alternately with cocktails 1 and 3. Before going away on holiday, spray with cocktail 3 and use a double dose of Dithane.
JANUARY	Summer pruning from middle to end of January. Pick blooms for the home. Check stakes and ties of Standard roses. Train climbing roses and tidy up by trimming side shoots that are in the way.	Follow your watering routine unless it rains. After long periods of rain, plants must be watered more often to acclimatize them once again to dry heat.	Fertilize at end of month as per September.	If rainfall is regular on the Highveld and Midlands, spray weekly, alternating with cocktails 1 and 3, and possibly 4. If it is very hot, check for red spider and spray at first signs of infestation.
FEBRUARY	Disbud Hybrid Teas and pinch out the centre bud of clusters of Floribundas. Continue dead-heading.	Follow your watering routine unless it rains.	Fertilize at end of month as per September.	Rain and dew bring on black spot, so spray with cocktails 1, 3 and 4, at weekly intervals if rain is frequent.
MARCH	Prize blooms can be exhibited at flower shows. Regular cutting of blooms and removal of dead flowers will assure continued colour until winter.	With the cooling of daily temperatures, watering can be reduced to once a week.	Fertilize at end of month as per September. In cold climates, use 3:1:5 as the last application of the season. If 3:1:5 is not available, use your accustomed brand.	Adhere to weekly spraying programme, especially at the Cape coast when it rains. Alternate cocktails 1,3,5 and 6 when the weather is damp – this will help retain foliage. If rust appears, spray with Plantvax.
APRIL	Autumn blooms are very colourful and beautiful and are a great joy at this time of the year. Cut back once the blooms are spent.	Plants should be kept moist by watering fortnightly.	In warm areas, fertilize at end of month as per September. In temperate areas, no more feeding is required until winter pruning.	Black spot is still prevalent and, especially during wet, rainy spells, spray plants regularly with cocktails 1,3 and 4 and 6.
MAY	Blooms are still being produced by the plant and they can be cut.	Water once every two weeks to prevent complete drying out and pre-winter dormancy.	In subtropical regions, fertilize at end of month as per September.	Black Spot is most active in cool conditions and should be controlled by spraying with cocktails 3 and 4.
JUNE	Depending on the climate, some roses are still growing, and should be left to do so. Others might have a short rest until winter pruning.	Keep roses slightly moist (water every 2-3 weeks). They can tolerate complete dryness for a period of time, as well as more frequent watering.	In subtropical regions, fertilize at end of month as per September.	Give yourself and your roses a rest.

Month-by-month guide to successful rose growing

part two

rose types

Rose growth types

Climber
Blossom Magic

Umbrella Standard
Ballerina

Standard
Iceberg

Shrub
Eglantyne

Pillar   Climber   Umbrella Standard   Standard   Shrub

54   Rose growth types

Hybrid tea
Madiba

Floribunda
Fellowship

Miniature
Minnie Pearl

Groundcover
Cream Sunsation

Hybrid Tea   Floribunda   Miniature   Groundcover

Rose growth types   55

Rose family groups

It is estimated that about 250 original rose species were in existence some 30 million years ago all over the northern hemisphere. For some 300 years now, however, hybridization of roses has been practised, to the extent that modern varieties are far removed in almost every respect from the original species. Today, about 50 000 varieties are grown around the world. Many of these are maintained in small numbers in rosariums, for posterity and research. In South Africa, it is estimated that about 3 000 varieties are grown, with a maximum of 1 000 varieties being offered for sale to the public by nurseries and garden centres.

Varieties

The correct terminology here is rose 'cultivar' (cultivated variety), which is a hybrid resulting from intentional cross-pollination. The term 'variety' denotes a natural hybrid – also known as a 'sport', as discussed below. For the purposes of this book, however, we use 'variety' as it is more commonly understood: as the condition of being diversified.

Rise 'n Shine, Miniature Rose

Major rose groups

Descriptive group names are assigned according to growth habit and use, and not according to shape or size of flowers.

Bush: This is the most common modern rose type of a more or less upright and neat growth habit, with a height of between 50 cm and 2 m and a spread or width of between 70 cm and 1,5 m.

Hybrid Tea: This defines both the traditional Bush rose growth habit, as well as flower shape – a high, pointed centre and unfolding spiral. Many Climber and Spire varieties also have the Hybrid Tea flower shape, but different growth habit.

Floribunda: These are Bush roses that produce flowers in clusters.

David Austin®English rose: Characterized chiefly by their flowers: full, double blooms of the older, pre-Hybrid Tea flower shape (cup-shaped or 'cabbage' rose) with an unusual fragrance and an informal growth habit.

Nostalgia: A selection of roses by other breeders, created in the spirit of David Austin®English roses.

Climber: Climbers produce long shoots and must be supported and tied to a fence, wall or pergola. Many David Austin®English roses and Nostalgia roses are also Climbers.

Colourscape: Varieties with an unusual growth habit – prostrate and spreading. They lend themselves to creating colour in landscaping, be it as Groundcovers of various heights, spreading Shrubs or Miniature climbers.

Miniature: Miniaturized flowers and leaves on plants of various sizes, ranging from tiny to 1-m-high Bushes, and small Climbers.

Pillar: The taller types of Shrub roses can be trained as Pillar roses by planting them next to a tall pole and fastening them to it.

Mathias Meilland, Floribunda

Rambler: Ramblers have a prostrate growth habit and, if left alone, will produce long shoots that crawl along the ground. Alternatively, they can be trained over a support many metres high, from which they will trail down gracefully.

Shrub: Shrub roses flower repeatedly and their growth habit ranges from neat to willowy. David Austin® English roses and Nostalgia roses are also represented in this category.

Spire: Spire roses grow upright to a height of 2 to 3 m and do not produce willowy canes.

For easy reference, rose names are listed in alphabetical order under their categories. A brief explanation of the name, relative growth habits and a comprehensive description of the shape of the blooms, colours and growth characteristics are included.

Rose names

Many modern roses have two names. The first name listed is the 'common name' by which the rose is generally known. The second is an international code, varietal name or denomination, similar to the botanical names of plants. These codes are derived from the first three letters of the name of the breeder, followed by his own code, e.g. **ESTHER GELDENHUYS** KORskipei.

This method of international coding avoids confusion. As they say in the Classics, 'A rose by any other name would smell as sweet', and some roses do indeed enjoy different names in different countries. For example, the rose known as 'Peace' in England, is called 'Mme A Meilland' in France; 'Gloria Dei' in Germany; and 'Gioia' in Italy. But if the name is coupled with an international code, then the rose can be identified by that code, even if its name is unfamiliar.

Protection

The breeder or originator of new rose cultivars can protect the rights of propagation of such roses. He can either secure a trademark on the name of the rose (indicated by an ® just after the name), or register the cultivar in terms of the Plant Breeders' Rights Act (indicated by an (N) just after the rose denomination). Such roses may not be propagated commercially without licence.

Height

The height a rose ultimately attains is dependent on soil, climate and cultural care, pruning and grooming. Since these requirements differ considerably from one environment to another, it is possible to determine only an approximate height for each plant. Below is an explanation of the terms used relating to height:

Compact – slight stature of 0,8 m
Medium – height of 1,2 m
Tall – height of 1,8 m
Very tall – any height between 1,8 and 2,5 m and over.

These heights are estimated at the end of the growing season and as from their second established year.

Hybrids

'Hybridization' is generally understood to be the genetic crossing of two different plant varieties within the same plant family. Whereas originally hybridization was left to nature – the wind and insects – man has deliberately been cross-pollinating roses since about 1870, resulting in the existence today, worldwide, of about 50 000 hybridized varieties. The approximately 300 new rose varieties that reach the market annually are selected from an astonishing three million seedling roses.

Salmon Spire®

Sports (Mutations)

'Sport' is the term commonly used for spontaneous mutations in horticulture. Sports are nothing new: the process is a natural phenomenon in the plant world. The 'Moss' rose, for instance, is a mutation of *Rosa centifolia*, and was discovered as far back as 1696.

How does this happen? In the process of cell division, a change might occur in a chromosome. If this is passed on to the daughter cell, it is possible that changes could take place in the morphology, resulting in a flower of a different colour, with a different leaf shape or a different growth habit. There might also be a change in the physiology: the rose might become recurrent instead of flowering only once a season, or there might be a change in the degree of hardiness.

Roses are most commonly prone to bud mutations, such as the sudden, whip-like growth from one cane of an ordinary bush rose. This has resulted in the development of a great number of Climbers, which produce very strong and extended canes, with flowering usually occurring only in the second year of growth. The blooms, however, are identical to those of the original rose. That is why they are known as Clg 'Peace', Clg 'Queen Elizabeth', Clg 'Crimson Glory' and Clg 'Sutter's Gold' etc.

The early 'striped' roses were all results of mutations. These days, far more sports are being released. One of the reasons is that cross-pollination of roses has led to many more hybrids with complex ancestries and vast gene pools that encompass every possible colour and shape of rose. Another reason is that private gardeners and professional rose growers have come to appreciate the commercial value of sports and are alert to any potential mutation that presents itself. The term 'sport hunters' has been coined – growers, who produce hundreds of thousands of plants of one particular variety, keep watch for any changes, and staff are also instructed to do so.

The most amazing sports amongst garden roses in South Africa are the offspring of 'Esther Geldenhuys'. A few years after its release, a gardener in Harare, Marie Cowper, realised that the deep-pink flower on her coral-pink 'Esther Geldenhuys' was a sport. She had the stem of this pink flower budded on an understock and, when the new blooms remained deep pink, she named the rose 'Lisa', after her daughter. She then had this rose commercialised by Ludwig's Roses in Pretoria.

Esther Geldenhuys, Hybrid Tea

Lisa, Hybrid Tea

An example of the Clg type rose. This is the Clg Cocktail

Soon thereafter, at Roeloffs' Nurseries, a cream bloom appeared in amongst a field of 'Esther Geldenhuys' plants. This rose was also budded and when it remained stable, Jan Roeloffs named the new rose 'Leana', after his daughter. Then, in faraway Swellendam, Nico Frick found a soft apricot bloom on his 'Leana' rose! This was budded by Duncan's Roses and eventually named 'Nicolette', after Nico's daughter. Recently, Nick Strydom, production manager of H de Leeuw & Sons Roses, found a red bloom amongst his block of young 'Nicolette' plants. This rose is named 'Vanessa' after his daughter. First prize, of course, will be a yellow sport of the amazing 'Esther Geldenhuys'.

Until recently, a sport belonged to the finder. Rose breeders found this to be unfair, and an amendment to the Plant Breeders' Rights Act all over the world now grants the right of ownership of a mutation to the breeder.

Although mutations can be artificially induced with the help of chemicals, or by irradiating budding eyes with radioactive isotopes, it appears so far that nature has been more successful with spontaneous mutations, which have proved to be more stable and thus of commercial value. It is also possible to use mutations in cross-pollination. Today, there are about two thousand commercial rose sports.

Leana

Nicolette

Vanessa

Standard roses

Standard roses are not trees: any rose can be bud-grafted at a chosen height on to a Standard cane. A Standard stem will not lengthen over the years, nor will it develop into a thick trunk, but will retain a balance in relation to the size of the crown.

Nurserymen select showy varieties with neat growth habit, and bud at a height that gives the best balance between length of stem and size of flowering head. Miniature roses are usually budded on 50-cm stems, Floribundas on 90-cm stems, Hybrid Teas on 1,1-m stems and Groundcover roses (which form an umbrella or weeping shape) at 1,2 to 1,5 m.

It is essential that a Standard rose always be supported by a strong stake. This might be a strong wooden pole treated with green chemical preservative (black creosote bitumen, especially if still fresh, is toxic to roots) or a suitable metal stake. The ideal metal stake will have either a T-bar or a ring welded to the top. When knocked in next to the rose, the top of the stake must be level with the crown, and not stop below it. In several places, stem and stake should be tied to one another, and some of the side branches of the crown should be tied to the T-bar or ring. Without support for the crown, strong wind can easily break it off at the top of the stem. It is essential that ties are checked regularly and renewed when they become brittle. Never use thin wire or similar material, since this will chafe the stem or grow into the bark, especially near the top. Stockings make good ties, and so do strips of rubber tube. The safest method of all is to wrap the stem and stake with a strip of shade cloth. It looks neat, lasts a long time and does not cut into the stem.

Standard Karoo Rose

Rose family groups 59

Bush roses

A Bush rose is the most common modern rose type of upright and neat growth habit, between 50 cm and 2 m high, and with a spread of between 70 cm and 1,5 m. The following classes are regarded as Bush roses: Hybrid Tea, Flora Tea, Grandiflora, Floribunda, a range of David Austin® English Roses, a range of Nostalgia Roses.

The enigmatically named Tea roses, the first 'everblooming' roses, are thought to have arrived from China in about 1850. They possibly carried the smell of tea, or had been packed together with tea, or the identifying document might have read 'Tea' or 'Thé'. The recipient called them 'Rose de Thé' – French for Tea rose. These frost-sensitive roses were soon cross-pollinated with hardy, spring-flowering European species, such as the Gallicas and Centifolias – producing Hybrid Tea roses. Efforts have been made to rename this group 'Noble roses' and, more recently, 'Large Flowering roses', but the popular name Hybrid Tea has survived.

Today, Hybrid Teas are the roses most popularly chosen for private gardens. They produce large, well-shaped blooms on strong stems, and are a good source of cut roses. A limited range of Hybrid Teas produces large flowers in clusters – the Grandifloras, the most famous being 'Queen Elizabeth'. Tall-growing and vigorous, they are ideally suited for a powerful colour display. Flora Teas are derived from crosses and re-crosses between Hybrid Tea and Floribunda roses, combining the best qualities of both. The well-proportioned plants are disease-resistant and extremely free-flowering, producing shapely, small but long-lasting blooms on medium-length stems. For a selection of Floribunda roses, turn to page 80.

ace of hearts

Hybrid Tea • medium
Large, scarlet-red blooms with extremely firm petals are individually carried on firm, strong stems. With such immaculate form, it is no wonder that blooms of 'Ace of Hearts' have been named champion at several shows in the last few years. They last extremely well on the plant and when cut. The bush is healthy, grows vigorously into a neat specimen of medium height and is clothed with deep-green, glossy foliage.

addo heritage

Hybrid Tea • tall
Addo is a small settlement in the Eastern Cape, well known for the Addo Elephant Park, but almost as much for the annual Addo Rose Show, organized by the local Women's Institute. This rose was named in appreciation for the prominence the rose has attained in that region. 'Addo Heritage' is unusual: green-pink guard petals protect round buds and, as they unfold into a symmetrical egg shape, a lovely coral pink is revealed which intensifies as the flower exposes layer upon layer of narrow petals, until the fully opened rosette shape of the old-fashioned rose is attained. When picked at the half-open stage, huge blooms unfold very slowly and will outlast all other cut roses. The bush grows vigorously into a tall, loosely spreading shrub, freely producing long-stemmed flowers from spring into winter. Can be planted to form a 1,2-m-high hedge.

alec's red

Hybrid Tea • medium

A dependable, high-performance variety, producing long-lasting, urn-shaped, pointed buds that open into large, full blooms. The clear cherry-red colour matures to carmine. The medium-high bush is robust, healthy, bushy and well branched.

ambassador

Hybrid Tea • tall +

Long, pointed buds open into large, shapely blooms; a cream-yellow colour on the reverse of the petals is overflown by the strong apricot of the inside petals. A tall, vigorous grower with long stems. The leaves are slightly sensitive to mildew.

andrea stelzer

Hybrid Tea • very tall

A superlative rose, named for the achievements of Andrea Stelzer, who won the title of Miss South Africa in 1985 and three years later the title of Miss Germany. Selected from the cut-rose trials, this clear-pink rose with extremely long stems and large pointed blooms was an easy choice. A bed of these roses presents a breathtaking sight, with hundreds of metre-long stems, each carrying a perfectly shaped bud or bloom. Long, pointed buds develop to reveal a perfect beauty with firm petals reflexing (curling outwards) and main-taining the sharply pointed centre. When planted closely together, the narrow, upright-growing bushes form tall hedges, with an inexhaustible supply of florist-quality cut flowers. The glossy foliage is mildew resistant. However, during rainy spells it is advisable to spray for black spot.

anna

Hybrid Tea • medium

'Anna' in full bloom easily gives the impression of a Floribunda because of its abundance of flowers. However, when the side buds are snapped off early enough, the remaining buds develop slowly into large, pointed blooms of a delicate cream-white that is brushed with pink as soon as the petals are exposed to the sun – and of superb exhibition shape. The vigorous, medium-height bush with bright-green foliage is extremely resistant to fungal diseases.

Bush roses 61

antique silk

Flora Tea • medium +

The favourite rose for bridal bouquets. As the petals of the rose are freed from tightly pointed, small buds, they curl at their tips, forming an open, star-shaped bloom of several layers with sharply pointed petals. Their substance and firmness enable the blooms to last for ages, be it on the plant or in a vase. The basic cream is enhanced by ivory-soft apricot spreading from the centre of each bud with a distinct silky sheen. The almond fragrance is a pure bonus. The bushes grow vigorously upright and produce a profusion of wiry, almost thornless stems. As this is a commercial florist rose, blooms must be cut regularly, small twigs removed and the centres cut out of candelabra stems.

belami

Hybrid Tea • medium

The outstanding overall performance of this variety is still underestimated. The medium-high bush produces masses of shapely, cream-pink blooms to appreciate in a vase, or on the nicely balanced and rounded plant.

bewitched

Hybrid Tea • tall +

Pointed buds open into especially attractive blooms of a clear phlox-pink colour with a strong fragrance. A tall bush, vigorous and healthy. 'Bewitched' is a dependable garden cut rose and a steady performer.

black madonna

Hybrid Tea • medium+-

Tight black buds open slowly, developing into shapely, medium-sized flowers with extremely firm petals. The deep velvet red of the half-open bloom glows in the sun and does not fade or change until the petals eventually drop. Carried on long, slender stems, they make ideal cut flowers. The bushes grow vigorously upright and flower profusely.

blue moon

Hybrid Tea • tall

This is the best known of the 'blue' roses. Pointed buds open into large, shapely, full blooms of a clear silver-lilac colour, with an overpowering fragrance. The plant grows tall and upright. It is vigorous, healthy and free-flowering with long, almost thornless stems.

boksburg fantasia

Hybrid Tea • tall

Brilliant, unfading tomato-red sparkles in the sun and is enhanced by a deeper velvet tone as the blooms mature. Long, sharply pointed buds open slowly into medium-sized, double blooms. The flowers are borne on long, straight stems as well as in candelabra-type clusters, ideal characteristics for outstanding cut flowers for the home, and a show in the garden rivalling that of a Floribunda. The bushes grow tall and vigorously and are clothed with healthy, green foliage. The slight but distinct fragrance is a bonus.

brigadoon

Hybrid Tea • medium+

Large buds develop into symmetrically shaped blooms with a high centre. The colour is basic cream-yellow with blends of pink, coral and orange appearing at stages of progressive exposure to sunlight. The dense bushes grow vigorously, and are covered with large, leathery, dull-green foliage. Disbudding is necessary in order to obtain exhibition blooms.

burning sky

Hybrid Tea • tall

The African sky has enchanted many, transforming its silver-blue hue into a fire at sunset. This rose is unequalled in its radiance of colour. Long, pointed buds open into large, exquisitely formed blooms. Shades of lavender, purple, bright pink and ruby red emerge at various stages as the flower opens. The blooms retain their colour and, as the petals fall, bursts of ruby buds are ready to take their place. Plant growth is vigorous, tall and bushy, with glossy, deep-green foliage. The classical Tea rose-shaped blooms are distinctly fragrant and produced on fairly long, strong canes.

bride's dream

Hybrid Tea • tall

White on pearl-pink, lace on satin, a new treasure lifts her veil for all to acclaim her beauty. The bud is long and bold, supported by a firm neck and provided with a carefully crafted filigree collar of five jade-green sepals. It opens slowly with delicate and well-timed precision. The 25 petals place themselves meticulously, one above the other, suggesting a marble sculpture. The mature, open bloom has the waxy, full-blown look of a water lily. The plant's growth is extremely vigorous, tall and prolific with long, elegant and practically thornless stems. Lush, healthy, moss-green foliage provides a royal carpet for the display. This is a bride's dream – as well as that of cut-flower enthusiasts. The 1992 *Rose Review of the American Rose Society* had this to say: 'No negative comments received. Colour and form draw almost every superlative in the dictionary.'

candy stripe

Hybrid Tea • medium -

One of the first striped roses to arrive on the market in the early sixties. It has shapely, pointed, medium-sized blooms of a basic soft pink with irregular stripes of carmine pink. A mutation of the old florist rose 'Better Times' from the 1930s, it has moderately vigorous growth.

colorama

Hybrid Tea • medium

Pointed buds open into star-shaped, medium-sized blooms. Each firm petal curls to a point at the margins. The reverse is cream-yellow; the bud unfolds to reveal cherry red on the inside, that changes to deep carmine. 'Colorama' grows to medium height and is moderately vigorous.

cora marie

Hybrid Tea • very tall

This rose will fulfil the ordinary gardener's ambition to grow long-stemmed cut roses. Each pointed, red bud is borne on an extremely long, slender stem and lasts very well, both on the bush and as a cut flower. The petals are so firm that the bloom in its half-open stage remains crisp for well over a week. The clear, red colour withstands even the hottest sun, without losing any of its velvet appearance and crimson glow. The plant is very vigorous and tall growing and the fresh, green foliage remains free of disease. Its enormous basal shoots are best staked in early spring to prevent them from snapping in storms and strong winds. This rose is sold by florists under its international name 'Dallas'.

casanova

Hybrid Tea • tall +

A proud child of the world's most famous 'Queen Elizabeth' rose. Pointed, large and full, the highly fragrant blooms are a strong straw-yellow colour that changes to cream. Blooms are produced in quick succession on a tall, vigorous, healthy and upright bush.

coppertone

Hybrid Tea • tall +

Enormous, pointed buds open fairly quickly into stunning, shapely blooms of gold-copper colour. Needs special attention to produce vigorous and prolific growth.

64 Bush roses

dainty bess

The Artistic Rose • medium +
Since its introduction in 1925, its charming clusters of single blooms have been captured by many painters. Pointed buds open into single, five-petalled curly blooms. Strong pink on the reverse of the petals is set off by delicate, soft pink on the inside, and by purple stamens and stigmas in the centre. Vigorous, upright, healthy and prolific growth. From its appearance, this rose should be classified as a Floribunda; however, when it was created there was as yet no such class, and the breeder released it as a Hybrid Tea. It remains the famous exception to the rule.

duet

Grandiflora • tall
Shapely, pointed, medium-sized blooms are borne in clusters and cover the tall-growing bush. The unusual tones of deep pink on the outside of the petals contrast with a lighter pink on the inside which is further enhanced by a deep salmon in the centre. Clustered flowering stems are popular with flower arrangers. 'Duet' is an excellent performer, vigorous and healthy with well-balanced growth.

duftwolke

Hybrid Tea
This variety is also known in translation as 'Fragrant Cloud' and 'Scented Cloud'. The shapely, pointed, double blooms are often of exhibition quality; warm orange to coral-red buds change to orange-pink in mature blooms. Vigorous, well-branched, healthy and prolific growth; rapid, repetitive flowerer. Its name is not an exaggeration of its capacity to sweeten the air around it.

egoli

Hybrid Tea • medium+
This vigorous rose produces large, firm buds, which open slowly into full, double, golden blooms with curly petal edges. The centre flower buds are mostly surrounded by several side buds, which also develop into large blooms – 'Egoli' rivals the best in Floribundas. For specimen blooms, disbudding is essential. Medium-high bush with large, dark-green leaves.

double delight

Hybrid Tea • medium +
Introduced in 1977, this spectacular rose has established itself as the most popular Hybrid Tea in sunny countries. Pointed, cream-coloured buds unfold slowly into full, double blooms; and, as each photo-sensitive petal is exposed to the sun, it changes to bright scarlet. As new petals unfold from the centre of the sizeable blooms, an unusual colour spectacle is created. During periods of overcast weather or when planted in partial shade, the colour conversion is not as dramatic. Deeply fragrant blooms are produced individually on strong stems and last well in a vase. The growth is medium high, vigorous, healthy and extremely prolific.

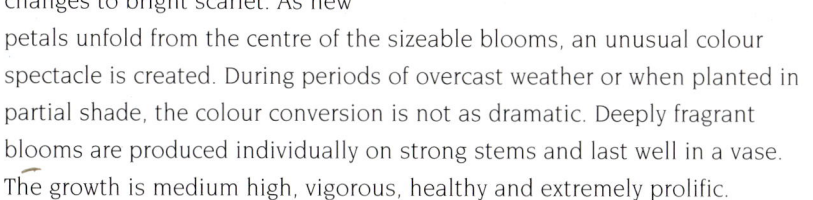

Bush roses 65

electron

Hybrid Tea • medium +

A very steady performer and popular rose since its introduction in 1969. Pointed, urn-shaped buds develop into large, fragrant blooms, which reveal their stamens when open. The colour is warm cerise-pink and growth is vigorous, rugged, healthy and prolific. An excellent, if very thorny, rose for any garden and specifically when grown on a Standard stem.

elegant beauty

Hybrid Tea • tall

Elegantly long, classic, sharply pointed buds, maintain their regal form for days thanks to firm, substantial petals. Added to elegance is beauty, captured in a most unusual pale yellow; at times enhanced by a faint suggestion of pink spilling over the petal edge. The bush, richly clothed in dull-green, robust, healthy foliage, is a vigorous, tall grower, that lavishly produces strong basal shoots. 'Elegant Beauty' is ranked among the top 20 exhibition roses in the USA and was elected to the *Hall of Fame* by South African gardeners in 1996.

elina

Hybrid Tea • tall

This creamy-primrose Hybrid Tea possesses classical beauty. Pointed buds open to reveal large, perfectly rounded flowers. The soft colour can be useful when 'hot' colours need toning down. It has been described as 'a rose to soothe the spirit and refresh tired eyes'. 'Elina' has proved itself to be extremely hardy and healthy; it thrives and performs with a minimum of maintenance and care. Growth is bushy and tall with abundant leaves of a medium-dark green.

esther geldenhuys

Hybrid Tea • tall +

Since its release in 1987 this rose has received wide acclaim for its performance, setting new standards for gardeners and florists alike. It combines vigour, a pleasing coral colour, superb shape of bud and open bloom and an ability to stay fresh on the bush and in the vase for a long time. Amazingly, it has sported (produced spontaneous mutations) four new varieties which are different in colour but have kept all its superb characteristics. These are 'Lisa', 'Leana', 'Nicolette' and 'Vanessa'. They can be planted together, making a spectacular show both on the bush and in cut-flower arrangements. The characteristic strong basals tend to form huge candelabra on their tips. To improve cut-flower quality, it is advisable to take out the terminal bud together with the next three side stems, which allows the lower stems to straighten and strengthen.

five roses

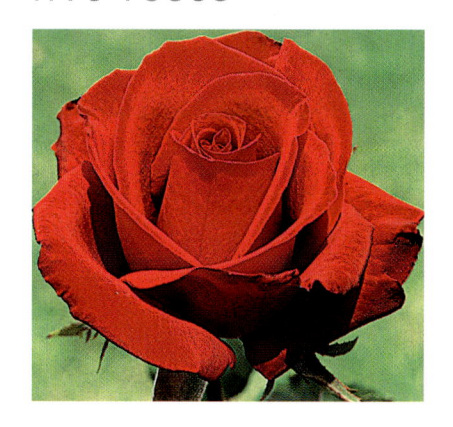

JACopper(N) • Hybrid Tea • medium+

This is not just another red rose: long, pointed, carmine-red buds stretch and develop to a perfect exhibition shape, with petals spiralling off an incredibly high, pointed peak. Very long lasting; the cardinal red develops a sheen of velvet on the inside of the petals. Vigorous, medium- to tall-growing bush with straight, strong stems.

germiston gold

KORtake (N) • Hybrid Tea • medium

1986 was the centenary year of the city of Germiston, where the first gold mine was started in South Africa. If ever a rose deserved to carry 'gold' in its name, this startling, truly golden Hybrid Tea does. The medium-sized, urn-shaped buds are sharply pointed and as the broad, firm petals unfold, slightly serrated, curly edges make the opening bloom specially attractive. The 30-petal blooms are symmetrical and without blemish, their deep-yellow colour holding its richness in the sun. The distinct, spicy fragrance comes as no surprise. The neat, even, medium-high growth is dense, and new flowering stems are continually pushed out all over the bush, giving colour for months on end. Being an excellent cut and exhibition bloom, it rivals the Floribundas for sheer floriferousness and quick repeating habit. However, old blooms do not drop and need to be removed.

flamingo

HERfla (N) • Hybrid Tea • tall

Beautiful, exhibition-sized, perfectly formed buds are a rich peach-blossom hue with tints of flamingo pink, and with a silvery reverse. These open into large, 11-cm-diameter, double flowers that last for days. The medium-high plants are vigorous and free flowering. A graceful rose.

golden monika

TANgolca (N) • Hybrid Tea • tall

Pointed, elegantly formed buds are carried on long, slender stems and make excellent cut flowers. The deep-yellow petals of the medium-sized blooms are firmly textured and ensure that the blooms last well. This tall-growing sport of the well-known 'Monika' is just as vigorous and healthy as its parent plant.

harmonie

KORtember (N) • Hybrid Tea •

If this Hybrid Tea does not allure you with its colour then it is sure to capture your attention with the whisper of its fragrance. Mix clear pink, subtle orange and soft yellow together and you have 'Harmonie's' colour – a shimmering salmon-pink. The bud is elegant and long. A tall, healthy, vigorous plant, bedecked with green, leathery foliage. Without disbudding, it performs like a Grandiflora, providing good cut flowers.

harry oppenheimer

KORabmask • Hybrid Tea • medium

It is no coincidence that the rose selected to honour Harry Oppenheimer has a playful combination of diamond green-yellow, maturing into deep gold. The stately, pointed buds are made up of firm petals that curve at the edges, and this lends them a certain elegance. The medium-high bush is vigorous and free flowering, providing a continuous supply of cut flowers and even exhibition blooms.

heike

KORrundum(N) • Flora Tea • medium-

The tight, firm buds have a green-yellow appearance that soon deepens into a clear, strong yellow. This colour is retained even in strong sunlight, as the petals unfold into shapely, full-bodied blooms. They are carried on sturdy stems that appear either individually or in candelabra. Without disbudding and deshooting, 'Heike' can compete with the best of the Floribundas for sheer flowering ability. In the vase, 'Heike' presents a challenge to all other roses. Vigorous bushes mature into neat, compact specimens that are astonishingly healthy and trouble-free for a yellow rose.

helen naudé

KORdiena • Hybrid Tea • medium+

Helen Naudé, with her lovely voice and refreshing approach, brings joy to listeners on Radio Jacaranda every morning. Now she is also a top exhibition rose. Seemingly fragile, delicately coloured blooms grace bushes of astonishing ruggedness and vigour. As the firm-textured, near-white petals unfold slowly from urn-shaped, pointed buds, they reflex and are brought alive with a soft coral-pink, brushed over the petals by sunshine. The perfection and symmetry of the blooms are revealed as row after row of petals unfold, a deepening coral contrasting and blending with basic white. These large, double blooms hold their perfect shape for a long time, be it on the bush, cut for the home or on the show bench. The bushes are extremely vigorous and grow into broad, densely branched specimens, clothed with bright-green, healthy foliage. Surely this is Mother Nature's own pride and joy.

ingrid bergman

POULman (N) • Hybrid Tea • medium+

Only a very special rose could honour Ingrid Bergman. Indeed, since its release in 1984, this has proved to be one of the 'great' roses. Bred in Scandinavia by the rose-breeding firm of Poulsen Roses, which has a century of tradition and experience, and whose roses are famous for their vigour and general hardiness – and 'Ingrid Bergman' is no exception. Thirty-five broad, firm petals make up the large, glowing, velvet-red blooms which hold their brilliance in the sun as no other crimson Hybrid Tea rose does. The bushes grow into well-branched specimen plants, clothed with glossy, deep-green leaves, which remain untouched by mildew or black spot. New bronze-red shoots appear until deep into winter, producing their shapely blooms in an abundance comparable to that of a Grandiflora rose. In April 2000, the World Federation of Rose Societies elected this variety to join 'Peace', 'Queen Elizabeth', 'Iceberg', 'Double Delight', 'Pascali', 'Duftwolke', 'Just Joey' and 'Papa Meilland' in the *Hall of Fame*.

johannesburg sun

KORdoubt (N) • Hybrid Tea • medium+

The deep-gold colour of the very long and sharply pointed buds softens as firm petals unfold into an open cup shape, releasing its distinct fragrance. The shiny bronze of the young foliage does not lose any of its gloss as it changes to a mature, deep green, remaining untouched by disease. Natural vigour ensures a continuous supply of blooms. It is sheer pleasure to grow this lovely rose anywhere.

joybells

KORsorb (N) • Hybrid Tea • medium

Green-tinted guard petals of the tight, urn-shaped buds reflex to display a rare cream-apricot colour. The petals unfold slowly to reveal a full, double bloom, with frilled edges. 'Joybells' grows into a medium-high, bushy plant, providing an abundance of pickable blooms. It is acknowledged as the best variety for drying blooms (with silica gel) picked at the half-open stage.

just joey

(R) CANjujo • Hybrid Tea • medium+

A good rose should be good everywhere. In local conditions, however, we do not get to see the deep coppery colour 'Just Joey' displays in the moderate European climate. But the subtle play of cream from the petals' edges to a darker shade of buff, down to copper in the deep centre of each bloom, is sufficient compensation. Indeed, the colour is so very variable that it is said there are two different strains of this rose. This is not so: the colour of the blooms simply reacts very quickly to changes in the soil or climate. Egg-shaped buds unfold slowly into large, double blooms, and the frilly edges of the firm petals add to the overall attraction. The bushes are strong and healthy, producing abundant, fragrant blooms, one to a stem. 'Just Joey' has become one of the most popular Hybrid Tea roses since its introduction to South Africa in 1978.

leana

ROELanda (N) • Hybrid Tea • tall

Being a sport of the popular 'Esther Geldenhuys', with the same vigour, superb shape of blooms and long-lasting qualities, it is only necessary to describe the colour, which is cream-white with distinct soft apricot rising from the deep-centred blooms as the buds unfold. This is a favourite rose for wedding bouquets.

limelight

KORikon (N) • Hybrid Tea • medium

Tight, pointed lemon-coloured buds mature into soft lime. In sunlight, the petals are brushed with a golden hue. Thirty-five waxy, firm, broad petals unfold slowly to form a classic, elongated, double camellia shape. 'Limelight' teases the nose with an unusual strong almond fragrance. Forest-green foliage glistens beneath the profusion of blooms on the well-rounded bush of medium height. Produces stunning cut flowers. Susceptible to powdery mildew.

Bush roses

lovers' meeting

Hybrid Tea • very tall

This rose lives up to its name, which suggests a colourful vibrancy and vivacity. Pointed, medium-sized buds are a basic Indian orange, which deepens to burnt orange as the unfolding petals curl into an immaculate star shape. Bushes grow tall and are clothed with beautiful bronze, healthy foliage. Planted as a hedge, 'Lovers' Meeting' will hide a 1,5-m-high fence with a continuous colour display as well as provide plenty of cut flowers. A virtually maintenance-free rose.

madiba

KORandpunk • Hybrid Tea • medium+

'Madiba' ('King' in Xhosa) is the name by which Nelson Mandela is affectionately known by South Africans. The 'Madiba' rose is strong growing. The pointed buds are deep maroon-pink, revealing a touch of yellow at the base of each petal. As the large blooms develop, the colour changes slowly to a deep lilac, taking on another hue of beige as the blooms eventually age.

maria callas

MEIdaud • Hybrid Tea • medium

Large, shapely blooms of rich carmine-pink. Vigorous, healthy and neat growth; a good performer.

maria therese

DOTrames • Hybrid Tea • medium

One of the finest exhibition roses recently introduced, bred by Simon Dot of Barcelona, Spain. Elegant buds open to form lovely, huge, full-bodied, 46-petalled flowers. The colour is an attractive deep orange-red, enriched by a flow of light vermillion. The plant is of a compact, bushy nature and bears flowers on strong, thorny stems.

marijke koopman

FRY Hybrid Tea • medium

This variety combines a clear, strong pink with exceptional perfection of bud and open bloom, and a vigorous, densely branched, healthy bush. It is a pleasure to grow in any garden and has become a favourite rose in a relatively short time in South Africa.

memoire

KORzuri (N) • Hybrid Tea • medium

From tight buds, firm petals unfold into large, shapely blooms that last well on the plant or when cut, and retain their pure white colour unblemished – even during adverse weather conditions. Remarkable for their hardiness and health, and their ability to carry blooms on sturdy stems at all times of the season. Listing the qualities of this rose cannot convey its superb, immaculate and reliable performance. This bushy rose is also suitable for growing in pots and on Standard stems.

mister lincoln

Hybrid Tea • tall+

Large, full-bodied blooms; rich red in colour with a velvet sheen. Strong and vigorous with many long, sturdy stems, and easy to grow. A classic, highly perfumed garden cut rose.

modern art

POULart (N) • Hybrid Tea • tall

Nature is given free rein in this display of colourful, impressionistic art. The basic, brilliant orange-red blooms of this new rose are brought alive by the contrasting white reverse of each petal. As the full-bodied blooms unfold, an amazing display of colour appears. These 'objets d'art' flowers are produced on strong stems, either individually or in small clusters, and in incredible profusion. The bushes grow quickly into tall, densely branched specimens, which withstand all weather and disease adversity with a smile.

mondiale

KORozon (N) • Hybrid Tea • Spire very tall

This is an extraordinary rose. Tall-growing, it provides extra-long stems of florist quality in abundance. The colour of the large, pointed, triangular-shaped buds and open blooms is a playful combination of deep coral-pink with a faint yellow that flows from the centre into each of the leathery petals. A slight fragrance is an added bonus.

The bush grows to 2 m, with many possible uses in the garden: as a flowering hedge when bushes are planted 70 cm apart, giving height behind other roses or breaking the monotony of walls when used in scattered groups.

mother's value

moon adventure

KORabemo • Hybrid Tea

Many of the most popular yellow roses have disappeared from the catalogues and nurseries: 'King's Ransom', 'Landora', 'Sunblest', 'Golden Fantasy', 'Spek's Yellow', to name but a few. Greater health and vigour are expected of modern roses and the 'yellows' are known to be particularly sensitive. Enter 'Moon Adventure' – strong, vigorous, tall-growing, free-flowering, with good, wiry, pickable stems and firm-petalled blooms. Its pointed yellow buds unfold slowly into double blooms of clear yellow, not unlike the full moon, and the colour holds well in summer. This rose needs only the minimum of maintenance.

KORreta (N) • Hybrid Tea • tall

Long-stemmed red roses convey ideas of romance and classy perfection. In the past, one had to depend on the florist; now a few bushes of 'Mother's Value' in the garden will produce such blooms. Buds are urn-shaped and sharply pointed, unfolding slowly into large, full blooms that hold the centre peak intact for many days. The colour is a spectacular, unusual, clear carmine-red. The plants respond well to regular cutting of blooms and to additional feeding.

Bush roses

myra stegmann

Grandiflora • tall

A gesture by friends saw the naming of this extraordinary novelty rose 'Myra Stegmann'. A descendent of the popular Grandiflora, 'Duet', this rose is its equal in performance, ensuring a never-ending profusion of shapely buds and blooms on a vigorous, stately shrub. Pointed buds open into charming, medium-sized, double blooms. It is, however, the colour that makes this rose special: a deep salmon-apricot that softens in the sun at the tips of the petals. A superb garden specimen, while loose arrangements of 'Myra Stegmann' will send admirers into ecstasy.

new zealand

MACgenev • Hybrid Tea • medium

For Sam McGredy to have named a rose in honour of his chosen home country, it had to be very special. Its strong perfume alone ensures this rose a firm place amongst modern roses. The foliage is leathery, glossy and very healthy. The bush grows strongly and is free flowering. Buds are pointed and globular, opening into large, very shapely, full-bodied blooms. In New Zealand's mild climate, they are indeed very large, a size they will also attain in our cooler climatic regions during autumn. The colour is a clear, soft, shell-pink.

nicolette

LUDswenic • Hybrid Tea • tall

This sport is, like sisters 'Leana', 'Lisa' and 'Vanessa', in every respect as good a performer as the mother plant, 'Esther Geldenhuys'. The colour of 'Nicolette' is not easy to describe: a mixture of soft apricot and buff, intensifying during cool weather, and softening in the summer heat. Excellent for cut flowers.

out of africa

KORocken (N) • Hybrid Tea • tall

A fitting name for this rose. Exquisite blooms combine the yellow, apricot and orange hues one associates with brilliant sunsets, simmering heat over the veld and that special warm and glowing feeling of Africa. The tall-growing plant renews itself with strong basal stems and large candelabras of perfect, pickable blooms.

oklahoma

Hybrid Tea • tall

A third hybrid that resulted from a cross between 'Chrysler Imperial' and 'Charles Mallerin'. The other two are 'Papa Meilland' and 'Mister Lincoln'. Large round buds open slowly into huge, full, highly perfumed blooms, with 55 petals of a deep velvet-red. 'Oklahoma' is a strong-growing, prolific and healthy bush with a well-rounded shape.

oyster pearl

® LAMrhowitch • Hybrid Tea • tall

An admirable sport of the proven 'Bewitched', it has the same unrivalled vigour of its progenitor, with shapely, full blooms carried one to a strong, upright stem. The colour is pale, cream-pink enhanced with a blush of deep pearl-pink flowing from the centre of the fragrant blooms over the unfolding petals. A good cut flower for the home.

peace

Hybrid Tea • medium+

One of the world's most popular roses, with over 100 million plants sold since its introduction just after the Second World War. Triangular buds open into large, full, pale-yellow blooms, rimmed with deep carmine. The deep-green, glossy leaves – a novelty at first – remain an attraction on the vigorous, medium-high growing bush.

pascali

LENip • Hybrid Tea • tall

Since its arrival in 1962, 'Pascali' has become one of the best white cut roses available. It is noted for its long, shapely buds and substantial blooms, which open in a most graceful manner. A healthy and prolific grower, and good florists' rose.

peace of vereeniging

® KORverpea • Hybrid Tea • medium+

Selected to commemorate the Peace Treaty of 1902 between the Boer Republics and the British Empire. This is a bold rose – in size, colour, growth and overall performance. The firm petals curl as they unfold from tight oval buds into full, double blooms of exhibition shape. The colour is a basic tomato-red with a golden reverse on each petal, at times overflown with red – a fascinating colour combination. The stately bush of deep-green foliage pushes up new, red-purplish shoots throughout the season.

Bush roses 73

people's princess

SUNtic • Hybrid Tea

A rose with a difference. Pointed buds, of an unusual, shy green-yellow tint, swell and develop slowly into large, firm-petalled blooms, when a strong pink appears and flows slowly from the petal edges towards the centre of the elongated, pointed blooms. The half-open blooms are of exhibition quality. Strong fragrance, no thorns, long peduncles that carry large blooms proud above the foliage, and general elegance are its royal attributes. The bush is vigorous and the leaves large and glossy.

potch pearl

HERtroci (N) • Hybrid Tea • medium+

It is appropriate that this free-flowering Hybrid Tea, bred by the late Jan Herholdt, was named after the town where he was born. Pointed, egg-shaped buds open into almost camellia-like double blooms with carmine-pink flowing over the petal edges towards the centre of the pearl-white base. Large blooms reach out from sturdy stems, with masses of deep-green, rugged, healthy foliage. A good cut flower, this rose also lends itself to group plantings and large beds.

pretoria

KORhagon • Hybrid Tea • tall

This new rose is able to produce multiple new stems, each bearing a long, pointed, cut-flower bud. In early spring, 'Pretoria' blooms a good week before most other varieties – a distinct advantage for exhibitors when the season is late. Buds open slowly into a loose wing formation, and are long-lasting, both on the bush and in the vase. The colour is deep red-pink, maturing into an attractive carmine. The fragrance is sweet and distinct. The tall-growing bush is clothed with lush, green leaves. 'Pretoria' also grows well in large containers.

pink crinolene

KORtrilac (N) • Hybrid Tea

This rose admirably combines the old with the new, and is aptly named for the graceful, wide-skirted dresses of yesteryear. Globular-shaped buds are carried on wiry stems and stiff peduncles, both singly and on huge, candelabra-like flowering spikes. As layer after layer of petals unfold, attractive, nostalgia-inducing blooms appear, silver-pink on the reverse of the petals, and glowing, deep pink on the inside, which intensifies in the sun. Despite their size and weight, these slightly fragrant blooms remain fresh for a very long period. They are excellent cut flowers. Healthy, deep-green foliage and inherent vigour ensure constant new growth and a steady supply of blooms. An almost permanent colour splash is created when a group of these medium- to high-growing, rugged roses is planted. They are excellent, too, among other roses in mixed beds, in hedge-like rows, or as individual specimens.

pridwin

KORmentoka • Hybrid Tea • medium +

This variety is vigorous, growing to above medium height. It has sturdy stems and produces very large, shapely, powerfully fragrant blooms in abundance – one per stem – with hardly any side buds. These are suitable as cut flowers and for exhibiting. The colour is strong mauve-maroon.

queen elizabeth

Grandiflora • tall+

This was voted the world's second most popular rose, after 'Peace', in 1979. Buds are pointed, medium-sized and unfold into large open blooms of clear pink. They appear in clusters and individually on long stems and are ideal as cut flowers. Tall and extremely floriferous, 'Queen Elizabeth' is found in virtually every garden, even where other roses do not perform. Ideal for background planting and for bedding.

red 'n fragrant

ORAdal • Hybrid Tea • tall

The name says it all. This is a rugged, vigorous rose that produces large, shapely blooms on super-long stems. The fragrance is powerful. Although the crimson-red of the bud and half-open blooms loses some of its glow when mature, it is certainly a valuable addition to red Hybrid Tea roses. The peak of the large, full blooms could be slightly higher for a perfect shape, but with a little dressing they are still suitable for exhibiting.

rina hugo

DORfury (N) • Hybrid Tea • medium+

Given the chance of having a rose named in her honour, Rina Hugo, South Africa's popular vocalist and an ardent gardener, selected a pink rose. But not just any pink: it had to be a trendy, deep magenta-pink. The blooms had to display the classical pointed shape. 'Rina Hugo' combines all that is essential in a rose: enormous size that still retains its elegant shape and fullness; a glowing pink that is quite different from any other pink rose; and a vigorous and strong-growing bush, in order to produce and carry such large flowers in rich abundance. A single specimen bloom in a vase will be a conversation piece.

shaleen surtie-richards

Hybrid Tea • medium
Shaleen Surtie-Richards – the famous 'Nenna' of the TV show, Egoli – was invited to sprinkle champagne over a mountainous arrangement of a clear coral-pink new rose, and officially give this variety her name. It originated from the all-time, deep-pink favourite, 'Electron', and matches that rose's ruggedness of performance, with large, shapely blooms and a strong fragrance.

stephanie de monaco

MEIpink • Hybrid Tea • medium+
Large, double, shapely blooms are carried on strong, rigid stems; an unusual combination of rose-pink with pale pink towards the edges of the petals. These attractive and very fragrant flowers appear in abundance on a neat, dense and well-branched bush.

sheila's perfume

(N)Hybrid Tea • medium
A cheerful red and cream-yellow two-tone rose that offers beauty, vigour and fragrance. The small to medium-sized flowers are elongated when young, opening wide to display pretty colours. Growth is bushy, upright and fairly dense, with particularly lustrous foliage that is reddish-purple when young

southern sun

(N) HERbeau • Grandiflora • medium+
Urn-shaped buds are borne individually or in large clusters and unfold into large, full blooms with attractive blends of gold, orange and red. The medium-high bush is vigorous and extremely floriferous, with slightly arched canes carrying heavy clusters of flowers. Very good for growing in containers and on Standard stems.

summer lady

TANydal (N) • Hybrid Tea • medium
Dignified, slender, velvety cream-pink buds speak of royal elegance and fine breeding. Long, firm petals unfold from the elegant bud displaying a deep, overlaid salmon tint welling up from the centre of the breathtaking bloom. The medium-high plants are well balanced, flower abundantly and are decorated with lush green leaves.

sun city

KORgater (N) • Hybrid Tea • medium+

It was only natural that this rose should be registered under the name 'Sun City'. The dazzling colour combination of deep yellow with luminous orange-red draws attention to the fashionably elongated, urn-shaped blooms held upright on strong stems. The petals are of such firmness that they hold their crisp shape into old age, until they are removed. The bush grows well, with maroon-red new shoots adding to the overall attraction. A show piece in the garden and an exciting rose for the flower arranger.

table mountain

KORnieoch • Hybrid Tea • medium+

These elongated, pointed blooms are shapely masterpieces with a most unusual colour combination: green-tinted guard petals enclose basic white blooms with distinct pink edges that are still touched with green. Extremely long-lasting, they are favourites among flower arrangers, both casual and professional. The vigorous, medium-high bush produces flush after flush of impeccable blooms on sturdy stems.

taubie kushlik

KORzinta (N) • Hybrid Tea • medium+

'Taubie Kushlik' combines the admirable qualities of its parents, 'Peter Frankenfeld' and 'Porcelain'. Firm, deep-pink petals unfold slowly from large, pointed buds, revealing a charming silver-pink inside that contrasts with the next layer of clear-pink petals in the centre. As the 35 broad petals unfurl and reflex, they produce a pleasing curl on the rim, making for a most attractive open, long-lasting flower. The rugged, vigorous, medium-high bush produces abundant blooms, one-to-a-stem, which last and last on the bush or in a vase.

tanned beauty

'ORAdon (N) • Hybrid Tea • tall

'Tanned Beauty' has long buds and elegant, half-open blooms with a sharply pointed centre of basic cream, and deep tan on the reverse. The tall and broadly growing bushes are vigorous and produce long-stemmed, highly perfumed cut flowers throughout the season. With a natural resistance to black spot, the foliage is not depleted by leaf drop, and the bush is able to flourish through periods of difficult climatic conditions. 'Tanned Beauty' is a companion, rather than a rival, to 'Just Joey'.

technikon pretoria

KORproa • Hybrid Tea • compact

The Technikon Pretoria has one of the largest campuses in the country, and sports the colours red, yellow and black. 'Technikon Pretoria' combines yellow with red, leaving black to the imagination. Firm, triangular buds of deep yellow expand as they develop, and as soon as the unfolding and reflexing petals are exposed to the sun, they turn bright red. As more petals unfold and overlap, the subtle play between these two colours is extraordinary. The bushes are very compact for a Hybrid Tea and retain a neat shape. Nevertheless, each large bloom is carried on a moderately long, sturdy stem decorated with large, deep-green leaves. New flowering stems appear at short intervals from early spring into winter. This healthy rose is superb for planting at the front of beds and in pots.

the lady

Hybrid Tea • tall

'The Lady' not only produces medium-sized, slender, long buds, but also tough foliage and a willingness to perform unperturbed during storm and sunshine. The colour is an unusual blend of yellow and pink. A tall-growing rose worth trying in your garden. It won the silver medal in the Durbanville Rose Trials in 1993.

tineke

(N) INES • Hybrid Tea • medium

True white cut roses are scarce and it is no wonder that this new rose from Holland has taken the florist market by storm. Pointed, full buds sporting a green tint open slowly into large, very full, shapely blooms of an almost immaculate white. They are carried on strong, straight stems and last extremely well. The bushes are robust and vigorous, producing abundant new stems.

touch of class

KRIcarlo • Hybrid Tea • medium

A French lady is always elegant, and 'Touch Of Class' is no exception. This is a special rose of classical form and long-stemmed blooms, with unique colouring of warm pink shaded with coral and cream. A vigorous grower that will present you with lots of flowers throughout the growing season. A 'must' for exhibitors.

Bush roses

vanilla

KORplasina (N) • Flora Tea • medium+

A florists' rose that has taken the European market by storm with its unusual colouring of vanilla with a distinct green patina. Smallish blooms are made up of numerous, hardy petals that unfold slowly and hold their shape for a very long time. The bushes are covered with robust leaves, in the fashion of old-fashioned roses. Grows well in all garden conditions and in large pots.

vera johns

KORvejoh (N) • Flora Tea • medium+

This acclaimed rose remains a personal favourite. Pointed buds unfold and stretch to a perfect star formation, which they hold for a long time. The colour is salmon, deepening into orange as the petals unfold. The bush is medium to tall, well branched, with hardy, glossy green foliage.

virginia

PEKwhina (N) • Hybrid Tea • medium+

The name implies a white rose, and indeed the large, shapely blooms of 'Virginia' are pure white (this is seldom the case, as most 'white' roses have a tint of green or cream). Exquisite flowers are borne in clusters and if left, will provide a show equal to that of a Floribunda. For cut flowers, remove side buds to allow the terminal bud to develop into a large exhibition specimen. The vigorous bushes are clothed with deep-green, glossy foliage which is astoundingly resistant to fungal diseases.

warm wishes

FRYxotic (N) • Hybrid Tea • medium+

Winner of seven international awards, including the coveted All American Award for 1996, this is generally such an outstanding, healthy and rugged performer that one risks overlooking the delicate beauty of the blooms. This hardy variety grows upright and produces shapely, fully petalled and fragrant blooms of an appealing, soft peachy-coral colour, providing excellent cut roses. One of the particular charms of roses is the evolving shape from bud to fully open flower. With 'Warm Wishes', this development is so slow that it takes weeks, rather than days, before the bloom has fully opened – and finally needs to be removed.

yankee doodle

® yanKOR • Hybrid Tea • tall+

Egg-shaped buds open into large, fully double blooms with many petaloids in the centre. A basic biscuit-yellow with blends of orange-pink intensifies to a sherbet-orange. The centres are often quartered, giving an 'old world' appearance. Healthy, profuse growth makes this easy-to-grow rose ideal for beginners.

Bush roses

Floribundas

These roses are remarkable for producing clusters of blooms, and flowering freely and continuously on hardy bushes. Although Floribundas are planted particularly for their colour display in the garden, the clustered stems can also be cut for informal flower arrangements.

The shape of the flowers may be single (five-petalled), semi-double (two to three layers of petals), star-shaped (firm petals reflexing from a pointed bud) or cup-shaped (numerous petals from a dense, quartered centre). The fore-runners of this group of roses were known as Polyantha roses and the next generations resulting from cross-pollination became known as Polyantha Hybrids. In the 1950s, well-known American rose breeder Gene Boerner coined the catchy name 'Floribunda' for promotion purposes, and it was soon adopted worldwide.

Floribundas should be planted 70 cm x 70 cm apart, and in single rows, 60 cm apart – and treatment is the same as for the other varieties. Keep in mind the height to which different varieties will grow when you are planning beds and rows. Think of the many spots these roses could brighten in your garden. They could create a neat hedge, become a focal point with a small group of plants or just a single specimen, hide the pool fence or simply create colour spots at eye level in front of evergreen shrubs.

bella rosa

KORwonder (N) • compact
Translated from Italian, the name simply means 'beautiful rose'. Certainly 'Bella Rosa' lives up to its name. Smallish, pointed buds are produced in such continuous abundance, that the super-glossy, deep-green foliage is often completely obscured by a clear-pink cloud of blooms. Flowers appear in clusters as well as one to a short stem, making them ideal for table decorations. The uniform, immaculate growth of these extremely healthy, maintenance-free bushes makes them ideal candidates for borders, group plantings and in containers.

bavaria

KORmun • Floribunda • medium
Semi-double blooms are striking velvet-red, with slightly curly petals giving a permanently fresh effect until they drop off cleanly. Neat, round, densely branched growth, with shiny, extremely healthy foliage. Should have a permanent place in every garden.

bavarian girl

KORleen • Floribunda • medium
Large clusters of semi-double, velvet-red, fragrant blooms cover the healthy bushes for most of the year. Wherever a real red is required, without a touch of orange or a hint of blue, 'Bavarian Girl' is the choice. The foliage is particularly attractive with its deep-green gloss.

bienkie

KORsisten • Floribunda • medium

This is a Floribunda to get excited about, not only because of its exquisitely shaped small blooms, but also for its neatness of growth and its floriferousness. The colour is somewhere between coral and apricot – soft, but still glowing and distinct. The small, tight buds consist of many crisp petals that curl at their tips as they unfold, holding the admirable shape of the open blooms for a long time. They appear in large clusters and as individual blooms on medium-long stems, and the long-lasting cut flowers make excellent table decorations. Its ability to flower from bottom to top makes 'Bienkie' especially endearing, and an ideal choice for planting in a large pot.

brilliant pink iceberg

Floribunda • medium +

This sport of 'Iceberg' was found in Tasmania in a private garden, and it is already very popular in Australia. It has the same extraordinary flowering characteristics of 'Iceberg', but the flowers are 'artistic', with various shades of pink splashed over basically white blooms.

bridget

KOReibei (N) • Floribunda • compact

Women of Peace had the charming idea of honouring their patroness, Bridget Oppenheimer, with her own rose: a deep coral-pink Floribunda that excels in neatness and compact growth and produces a never-ending supply of full, open blooms. Suitable for a neat ever-blooming border, for that touch of colour in a rockery, in front of taller plants or in containers on sunny patios.

carefree wonder

MEIpicta(N) • Floribunda • tall

Truly impressive. The young plant develops into a large, round, neat shrub of about 1,5 m in height and as wide, at all stages producing cluster after cluster of attractive candy-pink flowers, softened by a white reverse of the petals. It is a vigorous, healthy rose that overcomes, without requiring spraying, any fungal infections that may occur during adverse weather conditions.

city of belfast

MACci • Floribunda • medium

Semi-double flowers of a striking orange-red with pointed petals give a curly effect. Vigorous, spreading, healthy and prolific growth. A personal favourite.

city of pretoria

KORseubel (N) • medium slight

Roses are no strangers to Pretoria, administrative capital of South Africa. Indeed, the first rose show was held here over one hundred years ago. This tribute to the city boasts large clusters of shapely buds that unfold slowly, displaying the firm, pointed petals of its semi-double blooms. The colour is a stunning, deep orange-apricot with cream on the reverse of each petal. The plants grow into well-rounded specimens of an even height and are most attractive. Well suited to pots, as border plants, grouped in beds or to brighten any dull spot in the garden.

collegiate 110

DICknowall • Floribunda • medium

Named in commemoration of the 110th birthday of the Collegiate Girls' School in Pietermaritzburg. The clear-yellow, semi-double Floribunda blooms appear in great abundance on a neat, medium-high, rounded bush. They are ideal for borders, edgings, to fill open spaces in front of shrubs and even in tubs and large pots.

courvoisier

MACsee • Floribunda • tall

Pointed, shapely buds and very fragrant blooms come in clusters or individually on a stem. An abundance of pleasing, buff, straw-yellow flowers often covers the glossy foliage of the vigorous, healthy, well-branched bush.

durban july

durbanKOR (N) • Floribunda • medium

The name evokes a pageant of horse racing, fun, colour and fashion, and gives a good idea of the spirit of this new beauty. Clusters of medium-sized, deep-golden buds continuously bedeck the entire bush. As they burst into maturity, they display new apparel of vibrant orange, and eventually scarlet-red. To accelerate the natural repeating ability, old, spent blooms should be removed regularly to make space for new shoots, which start developing below the colourful petal umbrellas.

elizabeth of glamis

MACel • Floribunda • tall-

Excellent shape of bud and bloom; a most pleasing salmon colour, with a golden base to each petal. It grows vigorously, very upright, is densely branched with healthy growth and an easy top performer.

fellowship

HARwelcome • Floribunda • medium
This great performer received the coveted All American Award in 1995, and will soon be counted amongst the best in Floribundas. The breeder, Mr Harkness, says: 'A tremendous rose, plant it with confidence'. The colour is somewhere between deep copper and bright apricot on a yellow base. The flowers are a good size, semi-double and made up of firm petals. The long-lasting blooms display their warm and pleasing colour in profusion all over the bush, dropping off cleanly when aged. The bushes are vigorous and healthy.

flower power

KORedan (N) • Floribunda
Winner of the gold medal in rose trials in Paris. This rose is a winner in South Africa, too. The bush is covered with flowers throughout the long season. The medium-sized, open flowers are a pleasing clear salmon-pink, exuding a very strong and sweet fragrance. The bush is continually sprouting short, sturdy, lush shoots covered with glossy bronze leaves that mature into a deep glossy green, ending in a cluster of flowers. It remains a neat, rounded plant with flowers from ground level upwards.

friesia

KORresia • Floribunda • medium-
Pointed buds slowly unfold, revealing the 25 firm petals of long-lasting, semi-double and slightly curly blooms. The colour is clear yellow that remains brilliant in the hottest sun. Vigorous, compact and healthy growth, on which short-stemmed clusters and individual blooms are constantly produced, thus never disturbing the balanced proportions of the bush. The consistency of the plant's shape, size, the colour of the blooms and the rapid repetition of new buds to replace dead blooms, make 'Friesia' an outstanding performer.

gnome world

JACpat (N) • Floribunda
This is a lovely, very compact rose for border plantings, in tubs or on rockeries. The open, almost single flowers of fresh coral-salmon dance charmingly all over the neat bush. The brown-red leaves of the new growth are an added attraction.

gold bunny

MEIgronuri • Floribunda • medium-
A deep-yellow Floribunda with blooms of a pleasing shape, and firm, almost unfading, petals. The neat bush is always covered with pickable blooms for table decorations.

Floribundas

goldmarie '82

KORfalt (N) • Floribunda • medium
Imagine Goldmarie, the girl in Grimm's fairy tales who is showered with pieces of gold, and you have a picture of this new rose. Deep-green, glossy, healthy (beetle-free) foliage on sturdy stems, soon branches to produce large clusters of semi-double, firm blooms. Their colour is deep, golden yellow, strengthened by a red petal rim. Viewed from a considerable distance, bushes in full bloom stand out from all other roses. The colour is held for a long time, until the petals drop off cleanly. In performance, 'Goldmarie' is comparable to the world-famous 'Iceberg'; in colour it has no equal.

gold reef

POULdom • Floribunda • tall
Imagine a bush covered with golden nuggets and you get an idea of the appearance of 'Gold Reef'. Even better is that these nuggets, which are in the admirable shape of rose blooms, are replaced as fast as you can pick them. The bush grows to a stately height of about 1,8 m and remains neat, renewing foliage and blooms in a continuous fashion. The double blooms, of medium size and a deep, golden colour, appear in small clusters or singly on a stem and are suitable for home decoration. This rose is virtually maintenance free, but for water and food.

huguenot 300

DELteb • Floribunda • medium
French rose breeders, Messrs Delbard, created an industrious performer with this rose, a living monument to the arrival of the Huguenots in South Africa over three hundred years ago. Shapely, salmon-orange buds often completely cover the lustrous foliage. Indeed, clusters can have as many as a hundred blooms at one time, with more flowering side stems rounding off the attractive, vigorous bushes. The only extra care these bushes need is support for the enormous sprays in spring, to avoid breakage in heavy winds. Should the bushes grow too tall in the season, simply trim them with hedge clippers: within days they will again be covered with new lush, red foliage and the next flush of blooms.

iceberg

KORbin • Floribunda • medium+
South Africa's most popular garden rose. Small, pointed buds are borne in pure white clusters. Vigorous, extremely prolific, bushy plant growth. One of the most important bedding roses for any landscaped park or garden, because of its abundant flowering habit and the universal appeal of neutral white. A susceptibility to black spot during moist periods is quickly overcome with new bursts of growth. By pruning lightly in winter, 'Iceberg' can be grown as a shrub of about 2 m in height. Incomparable when grown on a Standard stem.

ivory beauty

KORivo (N) • Floribunda • medium

Such elegance of bud and bloom is seldom found in a Floribunda rose. The medium-sized buds are urn-shaped and sharply pointed before unfolding into delicate, semi-double blooms. Their soft, cream-ivory colour is enhanced by glossy, deepgreen, very healthy foliage on medum-high, well-rounded bushes. 'Ivory Beauty' will give softness against dark-coloured brick walls, in front of evergreen shrubs, in mixed rose beds, in large groups and in tubs. The fragrant blooms make good cut flowers.

karoo rose

POULkaros(N) • Floribunda • medium+

The Karoo: a long, hot, inland stretch of semi-desert? Those who really know the Karoo tell of its rich cultural legacy, interesting plant life, wonderful people – and its heritage of splendid roses. The colour is variously described as 'a summer sunset in the Karoo mixed with cool, fresh water-melon' or as 'crushed strawberry' – but it is not as simple as that. Buds start as deep orange-red, lighten into a strawberry-red in the shapely half-open stage, and finally pale to the colour of a cool watermelon, after which the petals drop off cleanly, without bleaching and looking unsightly. The bush grows easily and quickly into a well-rounded specimen, clothed with dark-green, tough foliage. Basal shoots as well as side shoots appear constantly, each carrying a cluster of shapely blooms. These not only perform admirably on the bush during the heat of summer, but are also excellent, long-lasting cut flowers for informal arrangements.

lava glow

KORlech (N) • Floribunda • medium-

Firm, double blooms are borne in large, tight clusters and carried on sturdy stems at an even height, their deep velvet-red never fading in the sun. Petals of elderly blooms drop off cleanly. Outstandingly healthy bushes with neat growth habit. Attractive new red growth matures into deep green. Should be planted in groups of at least three plants, or in single rows when the neatness of growth will enhance the compelling colour.

little pink hedge

Floribunda • medium

A sport of the amazing 'Little Red Hedge' and its equal in performance. It also bears huge, delphinium-like spikes, but in a clear pink. Indeed, when planted in a row, bushes will form a charming, ever-blooming low hedge. The glossy foliage is healthy.

Floribundas

mathias meilland

MEIfolio (N) • Floribunda • medium

A Floribunda that excels with large, continuously forming clusters. The bright-red, semi-double flowers contrast well with the shiny, deep-green foliage.

orange sensation

RUI • Floribunda • medium

This specimen produces clusters of semi-double blooms of a warm and luminous orange. The bush is vigorous and healthy, and ensures a continuous supply of flowers. A great performer.

nicole

KORicole • Floribunda • medium+

Basic white is really brought alive with shades of carmine, ranging from pale to intense, on the margin of each petal, softening as it flows over the exposed petals. Shapely buds, opening slowly into large, semi-double blooms, are borne in large clusters. Lush basal stems ensure a never-ending supply of fresh flowers.

naas botha

TANrosilb • Floribunda • medium-

Naas Botha, South Africa's rugby supremo, chose this lovely pink Floribunda to carry his name. It grows into a neat, compact bush covered with healthy leaves and soft-pink, fragrant buds with a silvery reverse. A charming rose, which is also known as 'Rosilba'.

pearl of bedfordview

MEIbeausi (N) • Floribunda • medium

Named after the garden jewel of the Reef, this rose impresses with its outstanding flowering ability. The pearl-white of the semi-double blooms is enhanced with a touch of pink that flows over the petal edges. A superb bedding rose where lightness and delicacy is required. Indeed, in the years since its introduction, it has proved to be one of the very best Floribundas available – for its vigour, health, floriferousness and beauty.

pernille poulsen

Floribunda • medium

An outstanding bedding rose with all the best Floribunda qualities. Clusters of semi-double blooms are produced in abundance in a clear, warm, salmon-pink. The bush is healthy, well branched, bushy and clothed with hardy foliage.

playboy

Floribunda • medium+

The lush, glossy foliage is a sight to behold, even before the first blooms appear. Of course, once the flowering season has started, there will not be a day that the bush will not carry at least some clusters of its charming, single flowers. The colour is basic yellow overpainted with layers of apricot and orange-red.

playgirl

MORplay • Floribunda • medium

The single blooms are a strong pink, with golden-yellow stamens. The five petals are firm and slightly curly, giving a fresh, lively appearance in the hottest sun. The value of this rose lies in its hardiness, and its ability to flower continuously, from the ground upwards, all over the bush. Such excellent habits make it very versatile, for landscaping, for edging rose beds, for tubs or mass planting.

rosehill

POULrohill • Floribunda • medium+

'Rosehill' surpasses all qualities expected of a Floribunda. The clear-pink blooms are semi-double, with several rows of firm petals that open slowly, hold well in the sun, and drop off cleanly as they age. The well-rounded bush provides flowers through all stages of development. 'Rosehill' is vigorous and repeats quickly. Outstanding as a hedge, a small group, or in mass plantings.

rainbow nation

DELstricol • Floribunda • medium

'Rainbow Nation' provides a riot of colour on a single bush, with endless colour combinations of basic velvet-red, yellow, pink and cream blooms. Every flower is different. Egg-shaped buds unfold into double blooms with firm petals that remain crisp for a long period. Not only is this a fun rose for its colours, but it also grows and flowers with ease, providing bunches of cut flowers. Glossy, indestructible, deep-green foliage is the perfect setting for such striking flowers. 'Rainbow Nation' is the most spectacular of the striped roses.

sandton smile

KORmetter (N) • Floribunda • medium

This rose would fit as well into the new category of Landscape roses – one of the reasons it was selected from many candidates to represent the up-market garden city, Sandton. Pointed buds half open into shapely, fragrant blooms that further unfold into curly semi-double flowers, at all times displaying a clear, soft salmon-pink. The bushes spread their huge clusters sideways to cover an area of about 2 m², making space for a continuous supply of new stems all carrying clusters of highly perfumed, pickable blooms.

satchmo

Floribunda • medium+

Large clusters of elongated buds unfold into semi-double blooms of dazzling, bright orange-red that deepens later in autumn. Vigorous, healthy and prolific growth; bears flower heads at an even height and is ideal for mass planting.

shocking blue®

KORblue • Floribunda • medium+

Medium-sized buds open into double blooms with 32 firm petals. The colour is not really 'shocking' or 'blue', but a rather unusual mauve-lavender in the bud stage, maturing into shades of silver-blue as the blooms are exposed to daylight. An outstanding cut flower that is stunning in arrangement with yellow blooms; the yellow 'Friesia' is an excellent foreground companion. Vigorous, healthy and prolific growth with new, deep-purple foliage and glossy, deep-green leaves. Highly perfumed.

springs '75

POULvision (N) • Floribunda/Shrub • very tall

Named after the Gauteng town of Springs to commemorate its 75th Anniversary, 'Springs 75' is a neat, shrub-like, floriferous Floribunda, bearing clusters of blooms all over the stately plant – an exciting rose that could transform a town into a colourful park. The mature bush is 1,8 to 2 m high, by 1 m wide. 'Springs '75' can serve as a pillar rose without a supportive pole, as background planting, as a specimen in the lawn, in front of evergreen shrubs, and is especially suitable planted as a hedge or screen, in rows 1 m apart. The pointed, 4-cm-high buds are of a light red to carmine-pink with 24 firm petals unfolding into 10-cm blooms. The strong pink changes into a softer, clear pink, without ever appearing faded. The petals drop off cleanly, adding to the general neatness of the rose. Stems with clusters of scented blooms can be cut in abundance at all times and enjoyed in the home. It is difficult to understand why this rose has not yet captured the imagination of the public, and is not planted in every nook and cranny as is done with 'Iceberg'. A star performer.

st andrew's

DICogle • Floribunda • medium

This is a charming performer, grown widely throughout South Africa, and gardeners' comments range from 'very impressed' to 'ecstatic'. Pointed, pink buds open slowly with overlapping centre petals, providing that 'old rose' look and hiding the stamens until the last, wide-open stage. These three distinct stages of development, the soft but clear pink colour, shapely blooms, sweet perfume, general floriferousness, vigour and neat growth habit have earned this rose high acclaim.

strilli

KORraffie • Flora Tea • medium

True yellow roses are rare. Pointed buds of clear yellow show no fading even at the wide-open stage. The bushes show vigour and excellent health. To be labelled a Flora Tea means an abundance of medium-sized, shapely flowers with firm petals on straight stems, and a good vase life. Indeed, each of the candelabra-type basal stems carries numerous shoots with individual blooms in addition to the many side branches, ensuring a continuous flow of colour.

zola budd

KORzola • Floribunda • medium+

Like the Bloemfontein athlete it is named after, this rose is delicate looking, but a sturdy grower, capable of blooming throughout the year. Once the long, pointed buds open, they last very well on the bush. The petals are a basic ivory with red and pink tones painted over the enormous, semi-double blooms. The bush is densely branched, very healthy and rugged, and lends itself to specimen and small group plantings, or as an impenetrable 1,2-m-high hedge.

striking

Floribunda/Shrub • tall

Open, semi-double, bright red flowers with a silver sheen on the undersides of the petals dance like butterflies on a vigorous, neat shrub of 1,5 m x 1,5 m. Use as a hedge or specimen shrub. Think of it as a red 'Iceberg'.

summer snow

Floribunda • compact

This rose, which has been around for about 60 years, could be described as a compact version of 'Iceberg'. Thornless, short stems carry clusters of open white flowers from early spring into winter. The bushes are always covered with blooms from ground to top.

Floribundas

David Austin® English roses & Nostalgia Bush roses

David Austin, English rose breeder, will one day be counted amongst the greats of rose creators. Obsessed with the charm of the quartered, highly perfumed blooms of old roses, with their graceful growing habits, and realising their shortcoming of producing spring flowers only, he set about developing a modified range of garden roses. He calls them, appropriately enough, 'English roses'. Other breeders were inspired to do likewise, and their creations, which reflect the spirit of David Austin® English roses, are identified as Nostalgia roses.

English Bush roses have the upright and formal growth habit of conventional Bush roses, e.g. 'Peace' and 'Queen Elizabeth'. They should be planted in beds or rows and can be mixed with Hybrid Tea and Floribunda roses. Their blooms are of the cup, quartered or cabbage shape associated with yesteryear's roses. Blooms are produced on good stems and can be cut, when fully opened, for arrangements. Petals of several varieties start dropping within a few days, particularly the fragrant varieties.

Winter pruning is carried out as with all other bush roses: thin out completely and leave three, or preferably four, basal stems, cut back to about 60 cm.

More David Austin® English roses can be found in the chapters 'Climbers, Ramblers, Shrub and Spire roses' and 'Floribundas'.

addo heritage

POULdotage • Nostalgia rose
This is a double-purpose variety, with flowers of the quartered, nostalgic shape of English roses, but whose firmness of petals and vase longevity rival the very best cut roses. A full description is in the Hybrid Tea section.

ambridge rose

AUSwonder • David Austin® English rose
Flowers are medium-sized, nicely cupped at first, opening to a loose rosette formation. A deep apricot-pink colour at the centre pales towards the outer edges of the bloom. This is a good all-round garden rose, flowering very freely and continuously, with neat, bushy growth.

belle story

David Austin® English rose
The large semi-double, silvery-pink blooms make a breathtaking spectacle. Wide open, with inward-curving petals, and a mass of stamens in the centre. Borne in huge clusters, they are produced prolifically all season long. The bushes grow upright to approximately 2 m high.

charles rennie mackintosh

AUSren • David Austin® English rose
Cup-formed flowers of a pleasing, distinctly lilac shade of pink, with a powerful fragrance. Produced with great freedom and continuity on a tough, bushy plant. An excellent rose for mixing with other colours.

fair bianca

David Austin® English rose
A pure white, strongly fragrant flower opening in the form of a cup, the petals gradually reflexing as the flower develops, exposing a neatly quartered centre. It forms a reliable, neat, compact bush.

bredon

David Austin® English rose
Numerous small flowers of full-petalled, rosette formation and a pleasing buff-yellow shade that changes to tones of apricot-pink as the blooms develop in the sun. Slender stems are sent up from the base of the plant, which quickly branch to produce a continuous succession of flowers on the 1,5-m-high plants. The clusters make long-lasting cut flowers.

francois krige

KORharment • Nostalgia rose
Named after the well-known artist and painter, the 'Francois Krige' rose is strong growing, reaching a height of about 1,5 m. Long-stemmed, huge, globular buds open slowly into quartered double blooms with the romantic appearance of old, 'artistic' roses. The crimson-red colour does not lose its bright hue in the sun, and firm petals ensure an extraordinary lasting quality, be it on the bush or in the vase.

David Austin® English & Nostalgia Bush roses

glamis castle

AUSlevel • David Austin® English rose

This is a charming white performer. Indeed, when the 60-cm- to 70-cm-high bushes are in full bloom, flowers almost completely conceal the leaves. Compact bushes produce flush after flush of clear-white, highly fragrant and typically double, open, cup-shaped flowers. These roses can be planted to form borders, in groups and in containers.

l'aimant

Nostalgia rose

This charming, medium-high growing rose has the characteristics of a free-flowering Floribunda. In never-ending supply, the double, salmon-pink blooms exude a powerful, sweet perfume. Indeed, the name links it with 'L'Aimant' perfume by Coty. It must have inherited its healthy, crisp and heavily veined foliage from its progenitor, 'Margaret Merril'. The performance of this novelty rose is most gratifying – it is a joy in the garden and makes the perfect gift for those who have romance in their hearts.

helpmekaar roos

KORogesa • Nostalgia rose

Described more fully in the chapter on Hybrid Tea roses, this rose can also be classified as a Nostalgia rose, with its double, open blooms.

magaliesburg roos

KORlasche • Nostalgia rose

This rose could well be classified as a Floribunda or even a Hybrid Tea. Globular, pointed buds unfold slowly into large, full, double flowers of the 'old rose' shape, and of a clear, deep-pink colour. They are borne in huge clusters and appear continuously throughout the season. The petals are firm and the flowering clusters make good cut flowers. The healthy, vigorous bush grows to medium height and can stand proudly as a specimen or amongst other roses.

prospero

David Austin® English rose
The compact, tough bushes should be planted in groups to achieve the full impact of the Gallica-type blooms, made up of numerous narrow petals neatly arranged in a perfect rosette. (Gallica roses were brought by the Crusaders from the East to Europe in the 12th century.) The colour is the richest crimson, turning into a beautiful shade of magenta. Moderate fragrance.

the prince

AUSvelvet • David Austin® English rose
Deep, rich crimson, quickly turning to a remarkable and equally rich royal purple. The pleasing flowers are of a cupped, rosette formation, and have a very rich 'old rose' fragrance. The bushes are relatively compact, growing to about 1 m high, and are clothed with dusky, dark-green foliage. They are vigorous, and rival the modern Floribunda in their ability to provide a show.

troilus

David Austin® English rose
Flowers are of an unusual honey-buff shade, the outer petals curving inwards to form an almost enclosed cup that later opens to expose a deep flower filled with a quantity of small petals. These have a sweet, honey fragrance to match the colour. Growth is sturdy, upright, flowering freely and repeatedly.

sharifa

AUSreef • David Austin® English rose
This is a very advanced and currently popular English rose. The highly fragrant blooms are shallowly cupped at first and gradually reflex to form perfect rosettes. Their colour is delicate pink fading to white on the outer petals, contrasting with the deeper pink revealed as the fully petalled blooms expand. These attractive blooms appear in large clusters on upright, firm stems, not unlike a modern Floribunda rose.

wife of bath

David Austin® English rose
A small, compact, tough little shrub that produces full, warm-pink, old-fashioned, fragrant roses continually throughout the summer into winter. Ideal for group plantings, hedges of about 1 m high, as single specimens or in large pots.

David Austin® English & Nostalgia Bush roses

Climbers, Ramblers, Shrub and Spire roses

These roses are of the long-limbed, spreading variety – and can either be left to organize themselves, or can be pruned and trained to fit in with almost any garden plan. Their security value should not be underestimated: here is the answer to truly decorative spikes.

Climbers produce long climbing shoots and must be supported and tied to a fence or pergola. For the best display, annual shoots should not be pruned or shortened, but tied horizontally.

Ramblers have a prostrate growth habit, and if left alone, crawl along the ground. Alternatively, they can be trained over a support many metres high, to hang gracefully down again.

Spire roses grow upright to 2 to 3 m and do not produce willowy canes. Their Hybrid Tea-shaped flowers make good cut roses. They are suited to tall background displays, in corners or as hedges, planted 1,5 m apart. If necessary, top the basal-stems at a height of 1,2 m to encourage branching and flowering.

Shrub roses flower repeatedly and their growth habit ranges from neat to willowy. They can be cut back or shaped at any time of the year and only need to be thinned out in winter. The taller types can be trained as Pillar roses by planting them next to a tall pole and fastening them with a strong rope. They can also be trained as Climbers on fences and walls.

altissimo®

DELmur • Shrub and Pillar-
Large, single, five-petalled blooms of brilliant oriental red are produced in abundance and repeatedly all over this exceptionally vigorous, healthy plant.

amber spire

KOR • Nostalgia • Spire
Large, globular buds are a deep cream, revealing intense amber colouring in the centre as the full, cup-shaped blooms unfold. The vigorous plant will stand freely with a slight arching effect. A perfect colour match with 'Just Joey'.

aperitif

Climber
Created by Sam McGredy of New Zealand, and perhaps one of the world's greats. 'Aperitif' is a climber with almost ideal growth characteristics and clear-yellow blooms of perfect Hybrid Tea shape, produced all season. Strong basal shoots grow to about 1,5 m, when they start to arch with the weight of the buds. Soon new shoots appear on the upper curves of the arches, each carrying a pickable bloom. This continues until it has reached a height of almost 3 m, unsupported. Trained on a pole or other support to arch downwards, it gives the effect of a yellow curtain.

ballerina

BENtal • Shrub and Pillar

Large trusses of single, small flowers in shades of pink, not unlike those of the hydrangea in both shape and colour. The plant has a vigorous, prolific growth habit; if unsupported, the long basal stems will give a willowy effect when weighed down by flower trusses. Flowers repeatedly.

blossom time

Shrub and Climber

Medium-sized, elegant blooms of cameo pink. Forms a 2-m-high, willowy shrub with vigorous growth that can be trained along a fence. One of the most floriferous and rapidly repeating climbers.

cecile brunner

Climber/Shrub

Miniature-sized 'button-hole' buds of a perfect, regal shape, of soft pink. It can grow into a large shrub with very thick main branches; can be pruned annually to desired shape and size. Blooms are borne continuously on side stems with long, delphinium-like spikes. Useful as a hedge rose.

blossom magic

MEInoiral (N) • Climber

A superb climber that can be trained to grow up poles and over walls, arches and pergolas, when it will trail gracefully downwards, flowering continually. Fairly large, double blooms are of a clear pink and are fragrant.

casino

MACca • Climber

Large, shapely buds open into full, double blooms of buttercup yellow with pink on the petal margins – not unlike 'Peace'. Vigorous, upright growth, with flowers in large, loose clusters at the ends of the long, strong canes. Glossy, healthy foliage. Blooms repeatedly.

clair matin

MEImont • Shrub and Pillar

Semi-double blooms carried in clusters throughout the season are of a shell-pink colour with golden stamens. Vigorous, healthy growth with many flowering side stems and tight clusters of blooms on the end of every shoot; forms a neat shrub with a willowy effect. Can grow unsupported or it can be trained up a pole or over a pergola.

Climbers, Ramblers, Shrub and Spire roses

cocktail

MEImick • Shrub, Pillar and Climber
Large, single blooms of crimson with a golden eye are produced in huge clusters. A profuse and continuous flowerer that carries its masses of blooms all along its strong basal branches and on the many side shoots; can be cut back during the season to keep in shape and to encourage a new flush of blooms. Freestanding or can be trained over a pergola or fence.

compassion

Shrub and Climber
This is a really tough rose. Unblemished by leaf disease, it performs outstandingly by growing into a huge 3 m by 3 m, self-supporting shrub, or as a climber when supported by a fence, pergola or pillar. The medium-sized blooms are of an immaculate Hybrid Tea shape and the firm-textured, delicate pink petals reflex as they unfold, revealing not only a pleasing apricot-yellow base, but also a very unusual, sweet fragrance. With new growth sprouting all the time and blooms appearing on each tip, be it a short side stem, or a lush basal shoot, there is never a time that this robust rose is without colour.

coral spire

KORkragor • Hybrid Tea • Spire
These flowers are perfectly shaped and sufficiently large to be superb exhibition blooms. The colour is a clear, distinct coral-pink. Growth is very vigorous and neatly upright with large, leathery, deep-green leaves for additional decoration.

crazy spire

Hybrid Tea • Spire
Shapely, Hybrid Tea-type blooms of an interesting combination of orange-red with yellow stripes and spots. The plant grows upright to 1,8 m and is slightly arching.

crimson glory

Hybrid Tea • Climber
Shapely buds and blooms of velvet crimson-red. Vigorous growth.

crimson spire

KORmiach • Hybrid Tea • Spire
Huge, crimson-red, shapely flowers are formed on long stems at different heights on this 2,5 m high growing rose. Blooms can be picked without exhausting the rose, since its astounding vigour ensures that it simply carries on growing and flowering.

don juan

Climber/Shrub
Large, Hybrid Tea-shaped buds are borne singly or in clusters on basal stems and side branches all season long. The full, double blooms are velvet-red. 'Don Juan' can be trimmed to a neat, 2-m-high shrub, or it does equally well as a climber when the branches are supported over a pergola or high fence.

double delight

Hybrid Tea • Climber
A climbing mutation of the famous Bush rose, with similar qualities: highly perfumed blooms of a basic white colour with a red edging flower in profusion the full length of the long climbing canes.

galway bay

Climber
Medium-sized, shapely buds of cerise-pink are produced on a vigorous, upright-growing, healthy climber. It can be trimmed to encourage new flushes of blooms.

Climbers, Ramblers, Shrub and Spire roses

golden showers

Climber, Shrub and Pillar
Medium-sized, shapely buds and semi-double blooms are produced repeatedly in large, loose clusters. The colour is a golden yellow that fades to cream as the blooms age. An exceedingly vigorous and healthy rose that can grow to a height of 5 m if supported. Foliage is glossy and profuse. This climber can be groomed and kept to size in the growing season.

handel

MACha • Shrub and Pillar
Shapely, medium-sized buds of cream, edged with rose-pink. Willowy, neat growth and glossy, healthy foliage. Flowers repeatedly and can be trimmed in the season.

iceberg

KORbin • Floribunda • Climber
Semi-double blooms appear in clusters of white, with yellow stamens. Very vigorous growth. Suitable for planting as a loose hedge, a large specimen shrub or trained over a pergola. Flowers profusely and continuously once the plant has matured, i.e. from the second season.

great north

DELgrord • Spire
The 'Great North' conjures up an image of high, snow-covered mountains – and this rose presents just such a show. Buds are pointed and well shaped, opening into fragrant, double white blooms. A mature shrub will reach 3 m and can be covered with over a hundred white, cut-flower blooms. Since this plant builds itself up with short, flowering branches rather than long, non-flowering canes, it is a neat Spire with wide use in free-form landscaping, especially along fences or as tall backgrounds.

Climbers, Ramblers, Shrub and Spire roses

iskra

Shrub and Pillar
Small, shapely buds open into semi-double, 'curly' blooms of bright crimson-red. 'Iskra' has a bushy but upright growth habit, and flowers profusely and repeatedly. A real showpiece when planted on its own.

joseph's coat

Shrub, Climber and Pillar
A highly prized shrub or climber rose. Medium-sized, shapely yellow buds open and change into orange-red and pink. The vigorous plant keeps on flowering as it grows into a willowy shrub or a wall-covering climber.

kordes brilliant

KORbisch (N) • Shrub
The dazzling brilliance of orange-red, double blooms on a hibiscus-type shrub is quite unique in roses. In just a few months, a maiden plant of 'Kordes Brilliant' builds itself up to 2 m high. Once the shrub has reached this stately shape, it is constantly garlanded with fiery blooms and glossy green, very healthy foliage. Planted as a focal point, a flowering fence or as a screen, this rose performs continuously without any undue care or attention.

mermaid

Rambler
This rose produces large, single blooms of pale yellow. Extremely rampant growth that can cover a pergola completely. Unchecked, it develops thick, woody centre branches. Glossy, healthy foliage. Flowers profusely and repeatedly.

Climbers, Ramblers, Shrub and Spire roses

peace

Hybrid Tea • Climber
Large, shapely blooms of creamy yellow with pink on the petal margins. Vigorous growth with very long canes, decorated with the typical glossy, green 'Peace' foliage.

rosa banksiae lutea

Rambler
The famous yellow 'Banksiae" rose. Except for the yellow colour, it grows and performs much the same as its white counterpart.

rosa banksiae alba plena

Rambler
Tight clusters of small, full, double, white blooms. Rampant, healthy growth; unchecked, it will grow into a very large specimen, covering complete fences and growing into trees. Needs only light pruning, or none at all, to retain flowering buds. The long canes are thornless. Flowers only once in spring, with occasional clusters in late autumn. A specimen growing in Tombstone, Arizona, is regarded as the world's largest rose: the main stem has grown, since 1885, to a thickness of 30 cm, and the rambling canes cover a pergola of 600 m^2.

rose celeste

DELroceles (N) • Climber/Shrub
Translated from French, 'Rose Celeste' means 'Heavenly Rose'. It boasts blooms of a shape and size expected only from a good Hybrid Tea rose. The colour is a blend of porcelain pink with a deeper pink on the reverse of the petals. However, whereas the climbing form of the Hybrid Tea rose flowers only once in spring, this rose produces fragrant blooms on the tip of every shoot throughout the season. Vigorous and extremely hardy, 'Rose Celeste' grows quickly to cover a wall, fence or pergola. It can also be planted without support, when it will shape itself into a naturally upright pillar. The more frequently blooms are picked, the more encouragement to flower.

salmon spire®

KORturnus • Hybrid Tea • Spire
The plant grows upright, producing long, flowering stems reaching to the sky, and eventually towering to a height of 2,5 m. Long, exquisite buds open as exhibition-shaped blooms of a lovely, clean salmon-pink, produced continuously and at different heights on the stately plant. They make excellent cut flowers. The strong fragrance is a pure bonus. When planted 1,5 m apart, they form a living hedge, providing not only a never-ending supply of cut flowers, but offering additional security. They are also useful as a freestanding background to rose beds or as individual specimens.

sutter's gold

Hybrid Tea • Climber
Long, pointed buds open to blends of yellow, orange and pink. Extremely vigorous growth with many long canes and shiny, dark leaves; unchecked, it grows into an enormous specimen that flowers profusely in spring and, to a lesser extent, throughout the rest of the season.

tullamore

Shrub
Smallish, shapely blooms of salmon-pink with a golden base. Neat, vigorous, upright growth. A charming specimen.

white spire

KORechtem • Spire Rose
Pointed buds appear in small clusters at the ends of long canes as well as on numerous short side stems. The colour is white and the fragrance inspiring. The plant grows upright and tall, ideal for background plantings or neat hedging.

Climbers, Ramblers, Shrub and Spire roses

David Austin® English roses & Nostalgia Shrubs and Climbers

As with David Austin® English Bush roses, these Shrub and Climbing varieties are characterised by the shape of their blooms – the quartered, highly perfumed blooms of old roses. These sumptuous blooms, combined with the graceful growth habits of Shrubs and Climbers, make this category of roses particularly appealing.

These varieties grow between 1,5 m and 3 m high when self-supporting, but long climbing shoots can be trained to a height of 5 m on walls, pillars and pergolas. Since they willingly push out basal shoots, winter pruning consists of removing older stems from the centre. Basal stems often grow to a length of 2 m and more. They can be pruned, or if left unshortened, they will arch gracefully and carry blooms along their entire length.

Once spring flowering is over, the main stems can be cut back to about 1.2 m, which will encourage a new flush of blooms. Alternatively, the stems can be shortened in winter, which will increase the length of the flowering stems and size of the blooms.

More David Austin®/English roses can be found in the chapters on Bush roses and Floribundas.

eglantyne

AUSmak • David Austin® English rose
The flowers are large and of an exquisite rosette formation; the petals turn up a little at the edges to form an almost saucer-like shape of soft salmon-pink, with a delicious fragrance. Growth is very vigorous, fairly upright to a height of 2 m, and slightly arching. Flowers appear all season long and all over the magnificent shrub. Although this plant is a superb freestanding specimen, it will also fulfil the function of a climber and a tall hedge. The dark-green leaves are slightly crinkly which adds to the overall attraction.

candida

AUSnun • David Austin® English rose
A rose with a difference. Deeply cupped, semi-double, white flowers, almost tulip-shaped, their stamens generally visible. 'Candida' grows into a spreading, slightly arching, many-branched shrub with attractive, slightly fragrant blooms appearing in clusters and individually all over the plant all season long.

golden celebration

AUSgold • David Austin® English rose

Very large, deep, cupped flowers of an unusual rich, golden yellow, and exceptionally fragrant. These magnificent flowers are held on strong, upright canes, which start arching at a height of about 1,8 m. The foliage is dark, glossy green which shows off the flowers to perfection.

graham thomas

AUSmas • David Austin® English rose

Lovely, cupped flowers of glistening yellow, filled with petals (like an 'old rose'), and with a strong scent. The bushes grow 3 m high on the Highveld and are self-supporting. Although they might spend their first year just growing, without many blooms, a good show can be expected the following spring, with a sprinkling of flowers throughout the summer and autumn. The leaves are healthy and make a good background in flowerbeds or on walls and fences. In the Western Cape it can be pruned severely in winter, and then it will flower profusely as a compact shrub in spring. The same applies to northern KwaZulu-Natal and the south-eastern Free State.

gwen fagan

POULgewfa • Nostalgia rose

A modern rose with the 'old look' has been named after Gwen Fagan, in acknowledgement of her tremendous achievements: collecting and documenting historic roses in the Western Cape, restoring them on some of the old wine estates and publishing a magnificent book describing and illustrating these glorious old roses. 'Gwen Fagan' grows into a stately shrub of 2 m, when the canes start arching, carrying clusters of large, double, fragrant blooms. Soon thereafter side stems appear, each carrying more flowers. The colour of the tight, double and quartered blooms is a deep rose-pink, fading to a lighter hue. This robust, healthy rose requires little maintenance.

john clare

AUSscent • David Austin® English rose

This compact shrub rose is a prolific flowerer. It bears medium-sized, informally cupped and half-open carmine-pink flowers throughout the long season. The neat shrub grows to a height of 1,5 m and has a lush appearance.

David Austin® English roses & Nostalgia Shrubs and Climbers

l d braithwaite

AUScrim • David Austin® English rose
The flowers open wide and are slightly cupped, brilliant crimson, with a good 'old rose' fragrance. The vigorous shrubs grow up to 1,5 m high and 3 m wide, and are covered with large blooms from spring to autumn, providing a wonderful show. Excellent as a bright foreground border to evergreen shrubs.

mary rose

AUSmary • David Austin® English rose
Large, fresh, rose-pink blooms that open to form a shallow cup filled with petals; they pale later without becoming dull. The strong 'old rose' fragrance is charming, but its real merit lies in the excellent habit of forming a robust, twiggy shrub that always branches to produce new flowers.

margaret roberts

AUSpale • David Austin® English rose
Margaret Roberts is South Africa's well-known herb lady. In ancient times, roses were very much part of the herbalist's collection, and it is fitting that this new rose be planted amongst herbs. Its excellent growth habit forms a robust, twiggy shrub that continuously branches to produce new flowers. These are large, soft pink in colour, with round buds that open to form a shallow cup filled with many petals. The strong, 'old rose' fragrance is its particular charm. In addition to being a marvellous specimen shrub, it can also be planted as a hedge, and can provide additional security if planted against a wall or fence. The flowers can be used to make potpourri or jams, and can be sprinkled in bath water.

molineux

AUSMOL • David Austin® English rose
This is a favourite among English roses, thanks to its outstanding performance. Neat and growing up to 2 m, this rose never seems to have a bloom out of place. They are neatly arranged all over the bush, and appear in rapid flushes of great profusion. The rosette-shaped blooms are light yellow, deepening into copper-yellow during the cooler periods of the year. They have a lovely, slight Tea rose fragrance.

olive

Nostalgia rose
The cupped blooms open into full, rosette-shaped flowers of unfading crimson-red. They are borne in huge clusters at the tips of strong arching canes as well as on numerous side shoots that appear throughout the season. 'Olive' will grow into a stately, huge specimen or give additional security when planted next to a fence or wall.

104 David Austin® English roses & Nostalgia Shrubs and Climbers

pat austin

AUSmum • David Austin® English rose
David Austin made the exception when he introduced a bright copper-orange variety. He named it 'Pat Austin' after his artistic wife. The large blooms are deeply cupped, enhancing the contrasting colours between the two sides of the petals. It grows to a vigorous 1,5 m, with arching canes and a multitude of fragrant blooms that glow amongst glossy, deep-green foliage. Can be trained as a climber on a support.

swan

AUSwhite • David Austin® English rose
Magnificent, large, white flowers (with just a tinge of buff in the early stages) are flat, even and rosette-shaped with slightly reflexing petals. The healthy, vigorous, continuously flowering plants are excellent as climbers or free-standing background plants.

sir edward elgar

AUSprima • David Austin® English rose
Prized for the beauty of its cerise-crimson colouring – the flowers are large and cupped at first, later developing into somewhat domed rosettes. The blooms are fragrant and the growth is strong and upright.

tradescant

AUSdir • David Austin® English rose
The neat, rosette-formed, medium-sized flowers are held in small dense sprays on the ends of arching canes. The colour is a superb rich wine-crimson, slowly turning to richest purple, and the scent is a powerful 'old rose' fragrance. The vigorous and healthy plants grow to about 2 m in height and arch admirably. They may be used as freestanding specimens, or hanging over fences and are ideal when trained over arches and pergolas.

winchester cathedral

AUScat • David Austin® English rose
In all aspects similar to 'Mary Rose', but with clear white blooms. A most valuable rose.

David Austin® English roses & Nostalgia Shrubs and Climbers

Miniature roses

Miniature roses originated from the Chinensis roses. Over the past 50 years, a few breeders have concentrated on cross-pollinating the original *Rosa chinensis minima*, cultivated in Europe since 1815, with a multitude of Hybrid Teas, Floribundas and even Climbers. This has resulted in an extensive range of varieties in virtually every colour and shape of bloom. Miniature roses are identified by their small blooms and leaves. Plants of some varieties can grow to a height of 1 m, and Climbing Miniatures are able to cover 3-m-high fences and pergolas.

Miniatures are 'everywhere' roses. They grow on garden tables, in old stone wash tubs, window boxes, pots around a bird-bath or in tiny townhouse or duplex gardens where one can simply take up a few flagstones in a paved courtyard and substitute good soil. Miniature Standards make beautiful backdrops for pathways or add colour to patio walls. To keep plants well shaped, they should be cut back twice a year (this can be done with hedge clippers) and they must be heavily pruned in winter. For best effects they should be planted in groups of about five, 30 cm x 30 cm apart or in beds, spaced 30 cm apart, with 60 cm separating rows.

Despite their Lilliputian stature, these are true roses with a rose's liking for a moist but well-drained root run and full sunshine for at least five hours every day.

anita charles

MORnita(N) • Miniature • medium+
The dusty, old-fashioned pink of the middle and inside petals and curled-back edges is backed and edged with rich ochre. The many, minute teardrop petals, each dusted with antique gold, unfold slowly, forming a classical, enchanting rose shape. The supply is regularly renewed by strong basal stems carrying candelabra of immaculate blooms. Numerous side shoots are clothed with leafy, dusty-green, hardy foliage throughout the season. Use for table decorations. Ideal in tubs, planters or on a short Standard stem.

amoretta®

amoRU • Miniature • medium+
Shapely, pointed buds unfold into large, double white blooms with a cream centre. Fully open, the blooms reveal attractive stamens. A densely foliated growth habit with few thorns; light-green, very healthy foliage. Flowers are produced continuuously, borne singly on slim stems, sometimes with several side buds. Can be thinned out and cut back at any time.

autumn magic

FOUmagic • Miniature • medium
This excellent little rose impresses with a profusion of buds and flowers of excellent form in a pleasing blend of yellow, gold, orange and red. Large clusters are borne on short stems, each producing a bunch of side buds, ensuring a never-ending supply of flowers. The bush is very vigorous but maintains a neat, rounded shape.

chasin' rainbow

SAVachas • Miniature
A compact, but vigorous, hardy little rose that is covered with lively blooms changing from deep yellow to orange, red and pink. Excellent for neat borders and containers.

fall festival

LAVfal • Miniature
The happy colours of an autumn party are all combined in each of the large, shapely blooms. The basic colour is bright tomato red, with yellow stripes patched and dotted all over each petal. The plant is vigorous and will grow into a substantial, round little shrub to knee height.

figurine

BENfig • Miniature • tall
Elegant, long, pointed buds of a delicate cream-pink open slowly into perfect, porcelain-like figurines, revealing a deeper tone of pink at the base. The bushes are vigorous and produce masses of long, slender stems.

gee gee®

BENgee (N) • Miniature • tall
A real charmer. Sharply pointed buds unfold gracefully into blooms of a classic rose shape. The colour is deep cream and even light yellow during summer, but in autumn, the blooms are suddenly transformed into admirable shades of apricot. The overall performance is astonishing. The bushes grow to nearly 1 m, and fill out on the sides almost as much. Slender stems are produced in great abundance and deliver charming, long-lasting cut flowers.

Miniature roses 107

good morning america

SAVagood • Miniature • tall

This vigorous, tall and dense-growing Miniature rose is never without long-stemmed cut flowers of a light-yellow colour. The buds are urn-shaped and open into exciting exhibition blooms when the light yellow intensifies, with pink and red on the petal edges. Use in pots, borders or small groupings.

little artist

MACmanley (N) • Miniature • medium+

A healthy, compact grower with dense, shiny foliage. The plant produces strong basal shoots, which develop into large trusses, creating a spectacular show when in full bloom. The Miniature, almost single blooms are white on the reverse and medium to dark red on the outer rim, slowly flowing into the cream centre of this star-shaped beauty. After a period of moderate weather, white veins run into the red of the petals, giving a 'hand-painted' appearance. Repeats very quickly.

lavender jade

BENalav • Miniature • tall

Few Miniatures have as powerful a fragrance as this attractive, perfectly shaped little rose. The pointed buds are silver-lilac and as the petals unfold, they reveal a deep lavender on the inside, giving the blooms a startling two-tone effect. The bushes grow well and carry long-lasting, fairly large, pickable blooms on wiry stems.

magic carousel®

MORroussel • Miniature • tall

Superlatively beautiful from bud to large, fully open bloom. White with pink on the petal edges. An extremely vigorous and healthy grower that produces an abundance of fairly long-stemmed blooms, and the longest-lasting cut flower. All in all, this is a most attractive plant and flower.

maidy

KORwalbe • Miniature • medium

Shapely, wine-red blooms with a white reverse are borne in never-ending profusion on a compact, densely branched bush. The healthy and vigorous plants do well as a border and in containers.

maverick

LAVsask • Miniature

Large, full blooms of an attractive basic red intermingled with white stripes and patches on each petal. If not regularly trimmed, the small shrub will grow to almost hip height.

minnie pearl

SAVahowdy • Miniature • tall

Delicate cream is tinged with salmon at the edges, which flushes over the exposed petals of the opening bloom. A most attractive and shapely bud with firm, reflexing petals is borne on a stiff stem and makes an ideal cut flower. The bush grows vigorously, is healthy and flowers profusely.

ocarina®

ocaRU • Bush • medium

Can be considered the best Miniature to date for all-round excellence. It has shapely, pointed buds that open into double, rosette-type blooms of a clear, warm, vermilion-pink. Vigorous bushes produce an abundance of new basal shoots with large, clustered flower heads, as well as numerous flowering side stems. Foliage is healthy, and shiny bronze when young. It performs impressively in any position.

peach festival

LAVcap • Miniature

Large, shapely blooms of deep, glowing coral are produced on sturdy, pickable stems. The bush is vigorous and grows into a substantial specimen.

picaninni

WRIpic (N) • Miniature

Des Wright, past president of the Federation of Rose Societies of S A, and an amateur rose breeder, created this new Miniature rose. The blend was shrewdly composed, and 'Picaninni' inherited the super-healthy, glossy foliage and sweet fragrance of 'Bella Rosa' with the bright orange-yellow tones of 'Little Jackie'. The truly miniaturised blooms are of superb exhibition shape. The plant grows vigorously into a fairly substantial bush and is covered with pickable stems.

Miniature roses

pierine

MICpie • Miniature • tall

A perfect Miniature companion for the Hybrid Tea, 'Esther Geldenhuys'. Urn-shaped, pointed buds open into deep, coral-pink blooms of classic rose shape. These are carried on long stems and make superb little cut flowers for table arrangements. The bushes are very vigorous and dense, growing to about 60 cm high and wide, and always decorated with masses of pickable blooms.

red shadows

SAVaspir • Miniature • medium+

An unusual garden variety with medium-red blooms that acquire darker shadings on the petal edges as they age. Extremely long lasting on the bush and in the vase. A compact, bushy, easy-to-grow plant.

rainbow's end

SAValife • Miniature

High-centred, Hybrid Tea-style, bright golden-yellow blooms with scarlet-edged petals make this an exhibitor's dream. The sturdy, wide petals open slowly. The plant is vigorous, symmetrical and compact, and is easy to grow, producing an abundance of flowers that are long lasting both on the bush and when cut.

raindrops

SAVarain • Miniature • medium

Here is another little charmer that captures and holds the eye. Lilac-purple buds and blooms are of superb exhibition shape and appear, in constant profusion, in clusters on lengthy, pickable stems.

ring of fire

MORfire (N) • Miniature • tall

As the round, yellow buds open, they reveal a touch of red on the tip of every narrow petal which intensifies as they unfold into fully double, pom-pom-type blooms, giving the illusion of a ring of fire. These vibrant blooms are borne on sturdy stems and last well on the bush until they eventually drop off cleanly. The bush is vigorous and covered with healthy, dark-green leaves.

southern delight

MORdashin • Miniature • medium+

The pointed buds and double flowers are a delightful blend of yellow, red and pink. The densely branched, vigorous bush is covered with flowers throughout the season. A welcome addition to the Miniatures from grandmaster Ralph Moore.

rise 'n shine

MOR • Miniature • tall

The best of the yellow Miniatures, with beautiful buds and large, double flowers of clear yellow, which are excellent for cutting and exhibiting. Free-flowering, healthy, tall, vigorous plants that should be pruned throughout the season by cutting all flower stems back weekly.

show 'n tell

FOUtell • Miniature • tall

This vigorous Miniature produces large, stunning flowers of an attractive, exhibition shape, in a two-tone display of bright orange and white.

spearmint

Miniature • medium

This is a cream-white sport of 'Ocarina' which is still considered our most prolific Miniature. The pointed, cream-white buds open into double flowers. Each of the multitude of new stems bears a cluster of these cream flowers, often hiding the foliage altogether.

Miniature roses

starina

MEIgabi • Bush • medium-
Buds and blooms are of perfect exhibition shape, oriental red brightening to orange with a slight yellow base to each petal. The plant enjoys vigorous, healthy and prolific growth, and excels in any position, especially in containers.

teddy bear

SAVabear • Miniature • medium
Aptly named, as charming, shapely little buds of deep orange-brown mature with a lilac flush over the teddy-bear colour. The bushes are easy to grow and are most prolific. Try one in a container near an open patio where you can admire it daily.

zephelene

KORkalba • Miniature
Perfect, relatively large Miniature blooms are a basic white that takes on a glowing coral tone as the petals are exposed to the sun; indeed, they are like 'little lights' as the name suggests in Greek. The bush is strong growing, maintaining a rounded shape, and is highly recommended for edgings, group plantings and in containers.

sweet symphony

MEIbarke • Miniature • medium
A Miniature rose from France, which has won the All American Award in its class. The bushy plant grows up to 50 cm high and wide, and is resistant to disease. Flowers appear in small clusters of two or three on short stems. The flower consists of 20 to 22 petals, in rosette formation. Cream-white in the centre with cherry-red edging, this rose makes a colourful display.

winsome

SAVawin • Miniature • tall
The bright, lilac-lavender blooms are exceptionally well formed, being full, double and high-centred, with thick petals of good substance. They are fragrant and long lasting, both on the bush and when cut. The bush is vigorous and productive, giving masses of shapely flowers.

zinger

Miniature • medium
A beautiful, semi-double rose on a vigorous, healthy plant. A profusion of pointed, bright-red buds open to brilliant crimson, shading to scarlet with a bright-yellow centre. This variety gives excellent value in the garden: it makes a splash of colour in a bed or a hanging basket. It also does well under artificial light.

Colourscape roses

Colourscape roses are defined by their unusual and informal spreading growth habit and not by the shape of their blooms, which can look like Hybrid Teas, or Miniatures, or be produced in Floribunda clusters. Most Colourscape roses are less subject to fungal disease and leaf drop than their more glamorous cousins, addressing a universal demand for low-care plants. Many of the new roses released every year thus fall under Colourscape or Informal roses. They require little or no spraying and hardly any grooming during the season.

Low Shrub or Informal roses encompass many Heritage-style plants, and grow to between 1,2 and 2 m, either arching their branches or filling out to a rounded specimen, flowering all over.

Midinette roses (Miniature Climbers) are particularly charming, with perfectly shaped Miniature blooms and foliage. Never overbearing, these shrubs fan out from the centre and may reach a height of between 1 and 2 m. They will arch gracefully over walls without needing support; form overhanging hedges; excel as specimens; or they can be planted in tubs. Prostrate Ground-cover roses hug the ground and shoots can stretch from 60 cm to 3 m and more. Basal stems arch under the weight of flowering trusses, increasing the spread of the rose. Eventual height may vary between knee and hip height. Continuous new growth provides flowers deep into winter.

apricot midinette

POULcot • Midinette • very tall
An apricot counterpart to the world-famous 'Cecile Brunner'. Perfectly shaped Miniature blooms of glowing apricot-orange cover the slender, arching stems all season. This rose will grow into a stately specimen, about 2 m high, and can perform as a climber on fences, in free-form hedges or in a tub. Glossy, red-brown stems appear all season long and the mature foliage is extremely disease-resistant.

baby love

Shrub 1,5 m
A most amazing rose that has won the President's Award in England. Bred by an amateur, it represents a breakthrough in rose breeding – a yellow rose that is extremely healthy. Expect the plant to grow in the first season to a respectable height of 1,5 m and about 1 m wide. It will be covered with charming, medium-sized, open flowers of a clear and virtually unfading yellow on a backdrop of deep-green, glossy, medium-sized leaves. Since this rose does not require any grooming or cutting off of dead flowers, it will form edible hips on a continuous basis. (Rose hips can be used to make jam or wine – it is claimed they contain more Vitamin C than any other fruit.) Many of these will be hidden in the forever-expanding bush, where they will ripen and turn red. 'Baby Love' will proudly stand on its own or in a group, grow into a neat hedge, or will dazzle in a large pot.

betty prior

Shrub
Clusters of cerise-pink, single blooms on neat, round shrubs. Does not make any long climber shoots, but builds the shrubs up to a size of 2 m x 2 m by means of its many sturdy, flowering stems. Blooms profusely and continuously.

clarissa

HARprocrastus • Midinette
These petite replicas of Hybrid Tea blooms, similar to 'Cecile Brunner', are deep salmon-apricot. Trusses can bear up to 40 blooms, so this is a superb cutting rose for small arrangements, especially where garden space is limited. Shrub grows 1 to 1,5 m high, slightly arching, and is covered with many shiny leaflets. Its upright growth suggests planting beside a pathway.

camilla sunsation

KORfibi • Groundcover rose
This Groundcover tumbles down slopes in a striking mass of energetic colour, a profusion of extravagant pink. Never shy, these bushes add joy and sparkle to any setting. Prostrate basal stems fan out to cover the ground completely, and blooms age without discolouration. This rose is adaptable: new basal stems are sometimes forced by dense lower growth to reach the light more or less straight upwards, and in such a way distort the groundcover effect. But as soon as space allows, the rose reverts to its distinctive prostrate growth pattern and the new shoots grow sideways again as nature intended.

cream sunsation

KORgarine • Groundcover • prostrate
A real charmer. Long, pointed buds open to large blooms with layers of neatly arranged petals of deep cream brushed with faint pink, fading to white. Growth habit is neat, compact and prostrate, arching if planted at the edge of a wall, in a pot or hanging basket. Superb as a Standard. Continuous new shoots ensure an endless supply of fragrant blooms.

crepuscule

Noisette- • Shrub and small Climber
Bred by Dubreuil in 1904,
'Crepuscule' quickly found its way
to South Africa where it is still
widely grown. Special qualities are
its hardiness, its abundant flushes
of near-double flowers, and its
attractive golden-apricot colour that
lightens to cream as it matures.
The plant sends out 2-m-long side
stems and will build itself up to a
1-m-high shrub if left unpruned. A
charmer on weeping Standards.

deloitte & touche

KORaucher • Groundcover rose
Charming clusters of yellow-, peach- and orange-tinted blooms form a knee-high carpet of colour. Warm-hearted, these rosebuds take on a lighter shade at the outer edges as they mature. This prolific and abundant rose is well suited to slopes, embankments and tubs strategically placed in the garden. Ideal for mass plantings that are expected to provide colour with minimal maintenance.

duncan's rose

Small Shrub
A deep-pink sport of 'Johannesburg Garden Club', with the same excellent growth characteristics.

fiery sunsation

KORtemma • Groundcover
The most exciting red Groundcover rose to date. Planted on a slope, it gives the effect of a low, rolling fire. Prostrate basal stems fan out from the centre, bearing their luminous, fiery red blooms at an early stage. These semi-double, fairly large blooms age without discolouring and drop off cleanly. New, short, glossy bronze stems are constantly activated to provide a continuous display of flowers. New growth is also extended sideways until an individual plant densely covers 1 m^2 with robust, healthy leaves and fiery colour. With its ability to renew growth from older wood, this rose needs little more than a trim to keep it at the desired low height. Can be trained to cover a swimming pool fence for additional security and colour.

Colourscape roses 115

jhb garden club

POULfan • Small Shrub

A lovely, neat Shrub covered with abundant delicate, single blooms of an exquisite soft coral, which dance like butterflies in the wind. Should hard rain spoil the delicate open flowers, it takes no longer than a day for new flowers to unfold. A hot favourite among gardeners for free-form landscaping and planting in pots and tubs.

memory bells

POUkleioma • Groundcover • compact

The plant builds itself up with short sideways-growing stems bearing dense clusters of flowers at the tips. Small, round buds unfold into pom-pom-type double blooms of clear, strong pink, with quartered centres. A superb rose that looks stunning in a pot or on a short Standard stem; healthy and needs no spraying to perform.

my granny

POULoma • Groundcover • semi-prostrate

This name was chosen to encourage families to make a gift of such a rose to a granny, or to plant one in remembrance of her. 'My Granny' has the charm of 'old roses' together with modern characteristics of vigour, health and continuous flowering. It is a spreading shrub covered with lush green foliage and the lovely, full, rosette-shaped blooms of yesteryear. The colour is a pleasing, clear pink. Basal stems soon form large clusters of blooms, and arch gracefully under their weight. New flowering stems are added and soon a 'rose hump' about 1 m high and 2 m wide is formed. Planted in a tub or budded on a high Standard stem, the flowering branches cascade admirably.

lavender midinette

MOR • Midinette

Of particular charm is the purple-lavender-pink hue of the pompom-like open blooms that contrasts strongly with yellow stamens in the centre. The attractive blooms appear in dense clusters on arching stems. The hardy plant grows into a small, willowy shrub 1,5 m high and about 2 m wide. The constant production of new stems ensures a continuous supply of colour and fragrance.

painter's palette

MORpale • Midinette

Nature's Picasso has had free reign here with its paintbrush! This little poppet's blooms are white, pink and red; and the variety and gaiety with which it displays these colour ranges on a single bush brings a whirl of colour into play. Tear-shaped petals fluff out, overlapping as in a multi-layered petticoat to form a neat, gay pompom. Soft moss bedecks the sepals. The plant grows into a 1,5-m-high shrub, and the branches arch outwards to occupy a space of 1,5 m^2.

queen mother

KORquemo

A super little Groundcover that produces semi-double, fragrant, pink flowers on prostrate, fan-like stems all season long. It performs in all sunny situations, and with little care other than watering and occasional trimming.

peach sunsation

KORommerla • Groundcover

Peach-tinted pompoms group themselves in attractive bouquets. This vigorous Groundcover, bedecked in a profusion of delicate colour, covers the ground with huge clusters of roses. The mature plants provide a knee-high carpet of colour.

pink sunsation

KORpinka(N) • Groundcover

This rose was awarded gold medals in the rose trials of Geneva and Baden Baden, silver medals in Kortrijk and Monza and a certificate of merit in St Albans, and it heralds the new generation of Groundcover roses. Overcoming previous shortcomings, 'Pink Sunsation's' ground-hugging, glossy, lush growth spreads out from the centre of the bush and quickly pushes out flowering side stems, until a sizeable area of about 1 m^2 is covered, decorated with charming, clear-pink, open blooms with golden stamens. Old blooms drop their petals before they fade, leaving an immaculate sensation in the sun. In shrubbery borders it will rival the performance of petunias or other annuals; in flower boxes, tubs, embankments or on a Standard stem it has no equal. Like other Sunsation roses, it can be planted next to a 1,2-m-high fence and with a little assistance, the canes will grow upwards, providing a flower wall of colour for most of the year, uncontested by any other rose.

Colourscape roses

rosy cheeks

MORsycheek • Mini-Shrub

This vigorously growing shrublet, which can reach a height of 1 m by 2 m wide, is not only covered with shiny, Miniature leaves but with hundreds of 'rosy cheeks' – semi-double, coral-pink blooms. Its ability to remain attractive at all times makes it a favourite in gardens, parks and landscapes. Apart from regular watering and feeding, it is quite maintenance free.

st katherine's

PEAvenus • Mini-Shrub

The colour is the deepest mauve-blue yet seen in roses. The plant is Miniature in terms of leaf and flower size, with arching branches that make it an ideal little shrublet of just over knee height that can even be used as a groundcover. Slender buds open into semi-double blooms, which exude a fragrance so powerful that it can be enjoyed even at a distance. Excels in containers.

sweet chariot

MORchari • Cushion Rose

One of the few Miniature roses that is highly scented. Very double, pom-pom-type flowers, in clusters of 5 to 25, in various shades of lavender, lilac and purple. This densely foliated bush remains neat and is ideal for permanent border plantings. Group plantings fill spots in rockeries or cover large areas in a garden. They are most rewarding in tubs or hanging baskets.

salmon sunsation®

KORpapie • Cushion • Groundcover

Imagine a large cushion embroidered with fluffy, double rose blooms of a deep salmon colour and you will have a picture of the stunning 'Salmon Sunsation'. These maintenance-free roses are suitable for borders and slopes, and in tubs.

summer morning

KORfullwind • Groundcover

This beautiful shrub is never without some of its semi-double, soft salmon flowers – and is often totally covered with them. The sideways-growing branches cover almost 1 m^2; the shrub continuously renews itself with lush growth from the centre, up to a height of 60 cm.

yellow butterfly

MORwings • Shrub

From a distance, yellow butterflies might be resting on the neat little shrub. Look closer, and you see an abundance of perfect, five-petalled, single blooms. Wave upon wave of blooms appear deep into winter. It excels in a tub, as a hedge, or en masse in huge landscape projects.

New roses

During the last three centuries, rose breeding has resulted in tens of thousands of new varieties. Not all of these have proved to be extraordinary, but a few have set new standards. Here is a small selection of some of the latest releases.

Even after thorough testing during the ten-year trial period from cross-pollination to release, a breeder cannot be certain as to how good a new rose really is. We now know that 'Crimson Glory', bred in 1935, represented a breakthrough in fragrant, velvet-red Hybrid Teas and today, all the popular red Hybrid Tea roses are derived from that variety. 'Peace', created in 1937 and released in 1945, was another breakthrough in terms of vigour, health and colour. 'Super Star' arrived in 1960 as the first vermilion-orange rose.

Although this variety was found to be susceptible to powdery mildew, it became the basis for the creation of a wide range of orange roses.

'Iceberg' was launched in 1958, but it was only about 20 years later that nurserymen and gardeners realised its true value.

Gardeners are inspired by the ongoing arrival of new varieties, and it is hard to imagine what rose growing would be like today had breeders not pioneered innovations like 'Peace', 'Super Star' or 'Iceberg'.

HYBRID TEAS

beach girl

Grandiflora tall • NEW
Produces huge clusters of perfectly formed Hybrid Tea-shaped blooms in a rich blend of peach, apricot and yellow. With vigorous, tall growth, and an ongoing supply of flowers, 'Beach Girl' performs with little care.

durbanville flame

Hybrid Tea • medium • NEW
Durbanville, a city just inland from Cape Town, is the proud host city of the Rose Trials which were established in 1981. 'Durbanville Flame' has the classical spiral exhibition shape of a Hybrid Tea and a striking peach-apricot colour that intensifies to orange at the petals' edges. Firm petals ensure longevity of the elongated blooms on the bush, and even more so as cut flowers. The bush grows willingly and produces firm, medium-long stems throughout the season.

garden queen

Hybrid Tea • medium+ • NEW
The incredibly huge blooms of this stately bush create a striking first impression. Of perfect exhibition shape, with pointed centres that hold for a long time, they are a blend of deep pink and violet and are strongly perfumed. The stems are sturdy and of medium length, well suited to carry the superlative, regal flowers. The leaves are deep green and robust. This queenly rose does not require any special attention to make a show of her royal breeding.

HP 2000

Hybrid Tea • NEW

Messrs Hewlett Packard are the main sponsors of the National Rose Convention organised by the Natal Rose Society. In appreciation, the 'HP 2000' Hybrid Tea rose was launched during the convention in September 2000. The large, full blooms are of a bold exhibition shape, having developed slowly from a pointed, urn-shaped bud. The colour is a glowing, deep peach-apricot and the fragrance is exquisite. 'HP 2000' grows vigorously to a medium-high, neat bush that flowers continuously.

leonidas

MEI • Hybrid Tea • NEW

Named after a Belgian chocolate, this is a novelty florists' rose. It requires special attention and regular spraying in a garden situation. It is bright orange with a golden reverse, while those grown specifically for cut roses, in greenhouse conditions, are a deep orange-brown. Those who have seen its blooms are challenged to grow this rose in their gardens – and a challenge it is.

patricia lewis

Hybrid Tea • tall • NEW

The popular singer, Patricia Lewis, selected a strong pink rose to be named in her honour. The glowing colour of the blooms hovers between deep pink and red. The sharply-pointed buds open slowly, spiralling to exhibition perfection. The thornless stems are long and strong and proudly carry the individual blooms upright, making them excellent cut roses. The foliage is a glossy brown when young, maturing to a shiny, deep green. The bush is vigorous and free flowering.

the rhenish rose

Hybrid Tea • medium • NEW

A rose named in celebration of the 140th birthday of the Rhenish Girls' High School in Stellenbosch in the year 2000. The choice is a rose of delicate cream-pink with petals spiralling from a high, sharp centre to impeccable exhibition form. The bush is vigorous and a prolific bearer of sturdy-stemmed cut flowers. Easy to grow in any garden.

zulu royal

Hybrid Tea • medium+ • NEW

At the request of the Natal Rose Society, a suitable rose was selected for release during the National Rose Convention held on 22 September 2000 in Durban. The choice fell on a most unusually coloured Hybrid Tea rose with a powerful fragrance. The colour is a blend of deep mauve with silver-lilac. The buds are pointed and open into large, symmetrical, exhibition-shaped blooms. The bushes are lively performers, growing quickly to chest height (1,5 m), and continuously providing pickable blooms. Francis Dorieux of France bred this new variety.

FLORIBUNDAS

Floribunda • medium+ • NEW

Some time ago, Ludwig's Roses singled out the SOS Children's Villages in South Africa as a favoured organisation for assistance and fund raising. This movement, which was started 50 years ago in Austria just after the Second World War, has grown into a worldwide organisation. A portion of the proceeds of every rose purchased will go to this deserving organisation. The 'SOS Children's Rose' is a happy rose that children will love. The colour has a chameleon-like ability to change from bright apricot-orange to a deeper tone of orange-red with irregular yellow stripes in the petals, and finally to age into a glowing blend of pinks. Medium-sized buds are long and pointed, and a profusion of petals prolongs the opening from tight bud to full-blown flower for over a week on the bush. The buds and blooms, which appear individually on medium-long stems, make excellent cut flowers. Strong stems carrying flower clusters branch out of the healthy, vigorous buss, ensuring a constant supply of colour. The 'SOS Children's Rose' easily grows to above-medium height, and is a good multipurpose rose: it can be mixed in with other roses, grown as a shoulder-high flowering hedge or planted in groups to create a focal point in parks and gardens.

sos children's rose

st john nonacentenary

Floribunda • medium • NEW

Synonymous with The St John Ambulance Foundation, this order celebrated its 900th anniversary in 2000. In appreciation for the Foundation's 'Service to mankind' and to assist in fund raising, a rose was named in its honour: a white Floribunda with a difference. The bush is hardy, vigorous and healthy, and flowers profusely, in dense clusters at the tip of each firm stem. White, pointed buds unfold slowly into shapely, open blooms, revealing a soft apricot-cream in the centre. At the point where other roses would shed their petals, the blooms of this novelty expand further to the next stage of a quartered centre, and finally the firm petals reflex downwards, creating the effect of an old-fashioned, immaculate white bustle. This excellent, multipurpose garden rose of medium height will supply an abundance of long-lasting 'spray roses' (cluster-flowering roses).

New roses

CLIMBERS

isidingo

ORAsapral • Hybrid Tea • Climber • NEW

In our search for new climbers that produce Hybrid Tea-shaped, pickable blooms and that flower more or less continuously from spring into winter, we were most impressed by a novel rose in our trials, bred by Messrs Orard of Lyon in France. The name suggested itself. The tight, full bud is green-yellow with an attractive rosy pink on the edge of each petal. As the bud expands and unfolds into a large bloom of extraordinary exhibition shape, the pink intensifies into a luminous coral, contrasting and intermingling with deep gold rising from the centre. The petals are slightly fragrant and firm, ensuring freshness and longevity. The foliage is robust, glossy green and an added attraction. Unsupported, this rose will arch at a height of about 3 m. Flowering stems develop all along on the strong, main branches, and the first spring flowers are replaced almost immediately with new blooms – a process that continues into winter. 'Isidingo' can be planted to stand without support, or with the main stem tied to the top of a pole or pillar. The main canes can be trained horizontally over arches or pergolas.

COLOURSCAPE

playmate

Miniature • Shrub • NEW

'Playmate' is a perfect rose for children, and appeals to the 'child' in every rose lover. It produces a profusion of minute, perfectly formed, golden-apricot blooms with a light fragrance. The growth habit is bushy with glossy green leaves. It grows to a height of 60 cm to 1 m, and needs at least six hours of sun a day. The blooms are pickable and the stems almost thornless, and can easily be handled by children. 'Playmate' is easy to grow, and does not require spraying against disease or leaf drop. It is suitable for growing in containers or in the garden, either massed in a bed or as a colourful, eye-catching border. This rose was developed to encourage children to care for, and contribute to, their environment - while having fun at the same time.

pretty lady

SCRIvo • Floribunda • Shrublet • NEW

'Pretty Lady' is difficult to classify – a supremely healthy rose with a neat growth pattern, producing clusters of large, shapely, soft-pink blooms throughout the season. It grows about 70 cm high and wide. The supple, flowering side stems ensure a very special display.

NOSTALGIA

adele searll

KORfaduv • Groundcover • NEW

Adele Searll, known for her charity work and her fight against drugs and narcotics, surrounded herself with beauty and flowers. The rose selected to carry her name in gratitude for her achievements, combines beauty and feminine softness with a busy energy that produces flowers continuously and profusely. Unfolded, the blooms are full and shaped like the centifolias of yesteryear, and with a petal count of 100. They measure 8 cm across, are sweetly fragrant, and an appealing apricot-pink colour. Plant growth is spread out, reaching knee height when the new canes arch from the sheer weight of their clusters of large, heavy blooms, suggesting graceful informality. The fresh green leaves are slightly rippled and remain on the bush until deep into winter. 'Adele Searll' is suitable in borders, in small or large groups, and it excels in pots.

garden and home

DELanac • Nostalgia • Bush rose • NEW

The 50th anniversary in 2000 of the popular gardening magazine, *South African Garden and Home*, was celebrated with the naming of a rose in its honour. The challenge was to find a variety that performs outstandingly in the garden and provides cut flowers to decorate the home. The 'Garden and Home' rose is one of the few roses that combines an informal growth habit and 'old rose' flower shape with the flowering ability and vigour expected of a modern variety. The flowers appear all over the plant, borne in clusters on upright stems. Round buds open slowly to a classical cup shape and, when finally fully open, display each of the numerous petals and stamens. The fragrance that escapes from between the firm petals is fruity and spicy. The colour changes slightly with each stage, from a distinctive pink bud and outer petals to warm shades of apricot and gold within the unfolding blooms. The bush has deep-green, slightly frilly leaves and grows to chest height. It can be planted in groups or rows or mixed with Hybrid Teas and Floribundas, or could grow in a large container.

MINIATURES

little nugget

Miniature • medium • NEW

This novel, free-flowering Miniature rose indeed produces little golden nuggets of perfect rose shape in great profusion, on a neat, medium-high plant. The deep-yellow colour does not fade, even in the hottest sun, and the buds make long-lasting cut flowers, ideal for exhibitors on the show bench.

New roses

Index of rose names

References to illustrations are in italic type.

A
Abraham Darby 14
Ace of Hearts *60*, 60
Addo Heritage 15, *60*, 60, *90*, 90
Adele Searll 15, *123*, 123
Alec's Red 14, 15, *61*, 61
Altissimo® 14, *94*, 94
Alyssum 'Snow Crystal' 20
Ambassador *61*, 61
Amber Spire 14, *94*, 94
Ambridge Rose 15, 21, *90*, 90
Amoretta® 14, *106*, 106
Andrea Stelzer 14, 48, *61*, 61
Anita Charles 14, *106*, 106
Anna 14, *61*, 61
Antique Silk *62*, 62
Aperitif 14, *94*, 94
Apricot Midinette 14, *113*, 113
Autumn Magic 14, *107*, 107

B
Baby Love *113*, 113
Ballerina 15, *54*, *95*, 95
Bavaria 14, 15, *80*, 80
Bavarian Girl *80*, 80
Beach Girl 14, *119*, 119
Belami 14, 15, *62*, 62
Bella Rosa 15, *80*, 80, 109
Belle Epoque 14, 15
Belle Story *91*, 91
Betty Prior 15, *114*, 114
Bewitched 14, 15, *62*, 62, 73
Bienkie 14, *81*, 81
Black Madonna 15, *62*, 62
Blossom Magic 14, *54*, *95*, 95
Blossom Time 14, *95*, 95
Blue Bayou 14, 15, 19
Blue Moon 14, 15, *62*, 62
Boksburg Fantasia 14, *63*, 63
Bredon *91*, 91
Bridal Pink 20, 21, 22
Bride's Dream 10, 14, *63*, 63
Bridget 14, 20, 21, *81*, 81
Brigadoon 14, 15, *63*, 63
Bright Smile 19, 23
Brilliant Pink Iceberg *81*, 81
Burning Sky 14, 15, *63*, 63

C
Camilla Sunsation *114*, 114
Candida 15, *102*, 102
Candy Stripe *64*, 64
Carefree Wonder 14, 19, *81*, 81
Caribbean 15
Caroline de Monaco 10, 15
Casanova 14, 15, *64*, 64
Casino 14, *95*, 95
Cecile Brunner *95*, 95, 113, 114
Charles Mallerin 72
Charles Rennie Mackintosh 15, *91*, 91
Chasin' Rainbow 14, *107*, 107
Chicago Peace 15
Chrysler Imperial 72
City of Belfast 14, 15, 19, *82*, 82
City of Pretoria 15, 19, *82*, 82
Clair Matin 14, *95*, 95
Clarissa *114*, 114
Cocktail *58*, *96*, 96
Colchester Beauty 14, 15, 20
Collegiate 110 14, *82*, 82
Colorama *64*, 64
Compassion 20, *96*, 96
Coppertone 14, 15, *64*, 64
Coral Palace 22
Coral Spire 21, 22, *96*, 96
Cora Marie (Dallas) 14, 48, *64*, 64
Coral Midinette 14
Cornelia 20
Courvoisier 15, *82*, 82
Crazy Spire *96*, 96
Cream Sunsation *55*, *114*, 114
Crepuscule 14, *115*, 115
Crimson Glory *97*, 97
Crimson Spire *59*, *97*, 97
Cupcake 14, 21

D
Dainty Bess *65*, 65
Deloitte & Touche *115*, 115
Denver's Dream 14
Don Juan 14, *97*, 97
Double Delight 14, 15, 48, *65*, 65, 68, *97*, 97
Duet 15, *65*, 65, 72
Duftwolke 15, *65*, 65, 68
Duncan's Rose *115*, 115
Durban July 14, 15, *82*, 82
Durbanville Flame 14, *119*, 119

E
Eglantyne *54*, *102*, 102
Egoli 14, 15, *65*, 65
Electron 14, 15, 48, *66*, 66, 76
Elegant Beauty *66*, 66
Elina 14, 15, *66*, 66
Elizabeth of Glamis 15, 22, *82*, 82
Esther Geldenhuys 14, *58*, 58, 59, *66*, 66, 72, 110

F
Fair Bianca 10, 15, *91*, 91
Fall Festival 14, *107*, 107
Felicia 20
Fellemberg 20
Fellowship 14, 15, 19, *55*, *83*, 83
Fiery Sunsation 23, *115*, 115
Figurine 14, *107*, 107
Five Roses 14, 15, *67*, 67
Flamingo *67*, 67
Flower Power 14, 15, 19, *83*, 83
Francois Krige 15, *91*, 91
Friesia 14, 15, 19, 23, *83*, 83, 88

G
Galway Bay 14, *97*, 97
Garden and Home *123*, 123
Garden Queen 14, 15, *119*, 119
Gee Gee® 14, *107*, 107
Georgie Girl 20, 21, 22
Germiston Gold 14, 15, *67*, 67
Glamis Castle 15, 22, *92*, 92
Glowing Achievement 19
Gnome World *83*, 83
Gold Bunny 15, *83*, 83
Golden Celebration 14, *103*, 103
Golden Monika 14, *67*, 67
Golden Showers 14, *98*, 98
Goldmarie '82 14, 15, 19, *84*, 84
Gold Reef 14, 15, 23, *84*, 84
Good Morning America 14, *108*, 108
Graham Thomas *103*, 103
Great North 14, 22, *98*, 98
Gwen Fagan 15, *103*, 103

H
Handel 14, *98*, 98
Hanneli Rupert 14, 15
Harmonie 15, *67*, 67
Harry Oppenheimer 15, *68*, 68
Heike *68*, 68
Helen Naudé *68*, 68
Helpmekaar Roos 15, *92*, 92
Heritage 14, 22
HP 2000 *120*, 120
Huguenot 300 14, 15, 22, *84*, 84

I
Iceberg 14, 15, 19, 20, 21, 23, 38, *54*, 68, 81, *84*, 84, *98*, 98
Ingrid Bergman 14, 15, *68*, 68
Isidingo 14, *122*, 122
Iskra 14, *99*, 99
Ivory Beauty 10, 14, *85*, 85

J
Janine Herholdt 14
Jennifer Joy 14
Joan Kruger 15
Johannesburg Garden Club 15, 115, *116*, 116
Johannesburg Sun 14, 48, *69*, 69
John Clare *103*, 103
Joseph's Coat 14, *99*, 99
Joybells *69*, 69
Jude the Obscure 14
Just Joey 14, 15, 48, 68, *69*, 69, 77, 94

K
Karoo Rose 14, 15, *85*, 85
Kordes Brilliant 14, 15, *99*, 99

L
L'Aimant 10, 15, *92*, 92
Lava Glow 15, *85*, 85
Lavender Jade 14, *108*, 108

124   Index of rose names

Lavender Midinette 14, *116*, 116
L D Braithwaite 15, *104*, 104
Leana 14, 15, *59*, 59, 66, *69*, 69, 72
Leonidas *120*, 120
Limelight *69*, 69
Lisa 14, 21, *55*, *58*, 58, 66, 72
Little Artist *108*, 108
Little Jackie 109
Little Nugget *123*, 123
Little Pink Hedge *85*, 85
Little Red Hedge 14, 85
Lovers' Meeting 14, *70*, 70

M
Madiba 10, 14, *70*, 70
Magaliesberg Roos 15, 21, 22, *92*, 92
Magic Carousel® 14, *108*, 108
Maidy 14, *108*, 108
Manou Meilland 14, 15
Margaret Merril 92
Margaret Roberts 15, *104*, 104
Maria Callas 10, *70*, 70
Maria Therese *70*, 70
Marijke Koopman 14, 15, *70*, 70
Mary Rose 14, 22, *104*, 104, 105
Mathias Meilland 14, 15, 19, *57*, *86*, 86
Mauve Melodee 19
Maverick *109*, 109
Memoire 14, 15, *70*, 70
Memory Bells *116*, 116
Mermaid 40, *99*, 99
Minnie Pearl 14, *55*, *109*, 109
Mister Lincoln 14, 15, *71*, 71, 72
Modern Art 14, *71*, 71
Molineux 15, *104*, 104
Mondiale 14, *71*, 71
Monika 14, 48
Moon Adventure 14, *71*, 71
Mother's Value 14, *71*, 71
My Estelle 14
My Granny 10, 21, *116*, 116
Myra Stegmann *72*, 72

N
Naas Botha *86*, 86

New Dawn 20
New Zealand 14, 15, *72*, 72
Nicole 14, 15, *86*, 86
Nicolette *59*, 59, 66, *72*, 72

O
Ocarina® 14, *109*, 109
Oklahoma 14, 15, 48, *72*, 72
Olive 14, *104*, 104
Orange Bunny 19
Orange Sensation 14, 15, 19, *86*, 86
Orange Sparkle 19
Oudtshoorn Joy 19
Out of Africa *72*, 72
Oyster Pearl 15, *73*, 73

P
Pacesetter 14
Painter's Palette *117*, 117
Papa Meilland 68, 72
Party Girl 14
Pascali 14, 15, 68, *73*, 73
Pat Austin 14, *105*, 105
Patricia Lewis *120*, 120
Peace 14, 57, 68, *73*, 73, *100*, 100
Peace Keeper 19
Peace of Vereeniging 14, 15, *73*, 73
Peach Festival 14, *109*, 109
Peach Sunsation *117*, 117
People's Princess *74*, 74
Pearl of Bedfordview 14, 15, *86*, 86
Penelope 20
Pernille Poulsen 14, 15, 19, *87*, 87
Peter Frankenfeld 77
Picaninni 14, *109*, 109
Pierine 14, *110*, 110
Pink Crinolene 14, *74*, 74
Pink Sunsation 20, *117*, 117
Playboy 14, 19, *87*, 87
Playgirl 15, *87*, 87
Playmate *122*, 122
Porcelain 77
Potch Pearl *74*, 74
Pretoria *74*, 74
Pretty Lady *122*, 122
Pridwin 14, 15, *75*, 75
Princess Alice 19
Prospero 15, 22, *93*, 93

Q
Queen Elizabeth 14, *44*, 60, 68, *75*, 75
Queen Mother *117*, 117

R
Rainbow Nation 14, 15, *87*, 87
Rainbow's End 14, *110*, 110
Raindrops 14, *110*, 110
Red 'n Fragrant 14, 15, *75*, 75
Red Rosamini 14
Red Shadows 14, *110*, 110
Rina Hugo 14, *75*, 75
Ring of Fire *111*, 111
Rise 'n Shine 14, *56*, *111*, 111
Rosa Banksiae Alba Plena *100*, 100
Rosa Banksiae Lutea *100*, 100
Rose Celeste 14, *101*, 101
Rosehill *87*, 87
Rosilba *see* Naas Botha
Rosy Cheeks 21, *118*, 118

S
Salmon Spire® 14, 21, *101*, 101
Salmon Sunsation® 21, *118*, 118
Samourai 15
Sandton Smile 14, 15, *88*, 88
Satchmo 14, 15, 19, *88*, 88
Shaleen Surtie-Richards 14, 15, *76*, 76
Sharifa 15, 22, *93*, 93
Sheila's Perfume 14, 15, *76*, 76
Shocking Blue® 14, 15, 19, *88*, 88
Shocking Sky 19
Show 'n Tell *111*, 111
Simplicity 14, 15, 19, 21
Sir Edward Elgar *105*, 105
Softee 14
SOS Children's Rose 14, *121*, 121
Southern Delight *111*, 111
Southern Sun 15, *76*, 76
Spearmint 14, *111*, 111
Spiced Coffee 14, 15
Springs '75 14, 20, 21, *88*, 88
St Andrew's 14, 15, 20, 21, *89*, 89
Starina 14, *112*, 112
Stephanie de Monaco *76*, 76
St John Nonacentenary 14, *121*, 121
St Katherine's *118*, 118
Striking 14, *89*, 89

Strilli 14, 15, *89*, 89
String of Pearls 10, 14, 21
Summer Lady 14, 15, 48, *76*, 76
Summer Morning *118*, 118
Summer Snow 14, 15, 23, *89*, 89
Sun City *77*, 77
Super Bowl 14, 15
Super Star 10
Sutter's Gold 14, *101*, 101
Swan 14, 22, *105*, 105
Sweet Chariot *118*, 118
Sweet Symphony 14, *112*, 112

T
Table Mountain *77*, 77
Tanned Beauty 14, 15, *77*, 77
Taubie Kushlik *77*, 77
Technikon Pretoria 15, *78*, 78
Teddy Bear 14, *112*, 112
The Lady *78*, 78
The Prince 15, *93*, 93
The Rhenish Rose *120*, 120
The Squire 15
Tineke *78*, 78
Touch of Class *78*, 78
Tradescant 14, *105*, 105
Troilus 15, *93*, 93
Tullamore 14, *101*, 101

V
Vanessa *59*, 59, 66, 72
Vanilla *79*, 79
Vera Johns 14, *79*, 79
Virginia 14, 15, *79*, 79
Vivaldi 10

W
Warm Wishes 14, 15, *79*, 79
White Spire 14, *101*, 101
White Sunsation 23
Wife of Bath 15, *93*, 93
Winchester Cathedral 15, *105*, 105
Winsome 14, *112*, 112

Y
Yankee Doodle 14, 48, *79*, 79
Yellow Butterfly *118*, 118

Z
Zephelene 14, *112*, 112
Zinger 14, *112*, 112
Zola Budd 14, *89*, 89
Zulu Royal 14, *121*, 121

General index

A

acid soil, neutralizing 11
alkaline soil, neutralizing 11, 24, 45
American bollworm 39, 42, *42*
anatomy of a rose *29*
aphids 42, *42*

B

black spot 41, *41*
blue, symbolic value of 12
branch, definition of 35
breeders' rights, protection of 57
budding on an understock 28, *28*
Bush roses 56, 60-79, 123
    pruning 34-6, *35*, *36*

C

chafer 42, *42*
Christmas beetle *see* chafer
clay soil, improving 11
Climbers 14, *54*, 56, 58, 94, 95, 96, 97, 98, 99, 100, 101, 122
    pruning 36-7, *36*, *37*
    training 37, *37*
CMR beetle 42, *42*
cold snap 46
colour
    affecting mood 12
    and fragrance, selecting roses by 14-15
    pigments 12
    the symbolic values of 12
colour wheel design 19
Colourscape roses 18, 56, 113-118, 122
conditions that suit roses 11
coniothirium *see* stem canker
container roses 47
    drainage 47
    fertilizing 47
    growing medium 47
    pest and disease control 47
    planting 47
    soil 47
    watering 47
containers 11
corner design 22
Cowper, Marie 58
Cushion Groundcover roses 113, 118
cut roses for the home 48
    arranging 48
    extending vase life 48
    guidelines for picking 48
    suitable varieties 10
cuttings, rooting 27-8
    hardwood cuttings 27
    softwood cuttings 28

D

David Austin® English roses 56, 90, 91, 92, 93, 102, 103, 104, 105
deadheading 31, *31*
deficiency diseases 45
Delbard, Henri 13
dieback 46
disbudding *31*
diseases
    deficiency 45
    fungal 40-2
downy mildew 41, *41*
drainage 24, 47

E

English Nostalgia roses
    Bush 15
    Floribunda 15
    Hybrid Tea 15
    Shrub 15
    Standard 15

F

Federation of Rose Societies of South Africa 49
fertilizing
    container roses 47
    roses 30-1, 39
Flora Tea roses 60, 62, 68, 79, 89
Floribundas 14, 15, *55*, 56, 80-9, 98, 121, 122
fragrance
    and colour, selecting roses by 14-15
    testing for 13
fragrant roses, selected 15
Frick, Nico 59
fruit chafers 42, *42*
fungal diseases 40-2
fungus attack, protection from 33

G

garden design
    for large gardens 18
    modern 16-18
    Victorian (formal) 18-23
Grandifloras 60, 65, 72, 75, 76, 119
green, symbolic value of 12
greenfly *see* aphids
Groundcover roses *55*, 113, 115, 116, 117, 118, 123
    pruning 38
growing medium for container roses 47

H

hail damage 33
harmful insects, beetles and mites 42-3
height of roses 57
Heritage roses 113
Hybrid Tea roses 14, 15, *55*, 56, 60-1, 62-7, 68-71, 72, 73-4, 75, 76, 77-8, 79, 96, 97, 100, 101, 119, 120, 121, 122
hybridization 57

I

'Iceberg', pruning 38
insects, beetles and mites, harmful 42-3
international coding of rose names 57
iron, lack of 30, 45, *45*
irrigation 30

L

light requirements 11

M

magnesium, lack of 45, *45*
Midinette roses 113, 114, 116, 117
Miniature Climbers *see* Midinette roses
Miniature roses 14, *55*, 56, 106-112
    pruning 37
month-by-month guide to successful rose growing 50-1
Moss rose 57
mulching 39
mutations *see* sports

N

names of roses 57
nitrogen, lack of 45, *45*
Nostalgia roses 15, 56, 90, 91, 92, 103, 104, 123

O

origins of rose 10
oval design 23

P

peanut beetle *see* chafer
pernicious scale 39, 42, *42*
pest and disease control 40-6
    container roses 47
pesticide cocktails 40, 43-4
    preparation of 43
    quantities 44
    recipes 44
pests 42-3
phosphorus, lack of 45, *45*
Pillar roses *54*, 56, 94, 95, 96, 98, 99

Plant Breeders' Rights Act 57, 59
planting 24-6
   bare-root roses 26, *26*
   Climbers *26*
   container roses 47
   in stony or rocky gardens 26
   Standard roses *26*
potassium, lack of 45, *45*
powdery mildew 39, 40-1, *40*, *41*
propagating roses 27-8
   budding on an understock 28
   rooting cuttings 27-8, *27*
pruning
   aftercare 38-9
   Bush roses 34-6, *35*, *36*
   Climbers 36-7, *36*, *37*
   equipment 34, *34*
   free-flowering varieties 32
   Groundcover roses 32, 38
   'Iceberg' 38
   light early-summer 31-2
   Miniature roses 32, 37
   reasons for 34
   severe 33, *33*
   Shrub roses 36
   shy-flowering roses 32
   specimen Bush roses 36
   Spire roses 36
   Standard roses 38, *38*
   summer 32-3, *32*
   when to 34
   winter 34-9

R
Ramblers 57, 99, 100
red, symbolic value of 12
red spider 38, 43, *43*
Roeloffs, Jan 59
rooting cuttings 27-8
Rosa centifolia 57
rose bed, preparing a 24-5, *24*, *25*
rose borer 39, 43, *43*
rose garden design, Victorian (formal) 18-23

colour wheel design 19
corner design 22
general rules 18
oval design 23
square design 21
square walk-about design 20
rose groups 56-7
rose growing, month-by-month guide 50-1
rose names 57
   international coding 57
rose oil (attar) 10
rose perfume, identifying 13
rose rust 42, *42*
rosewater 11

S
sandy soil, upgrading 11
scented roses, thoughts on 13
Shrub roses (small) 113, 114, 115, 116, 118
Shrub roses *54*, 57, 94, 95, 96, 97, 98, 99, 101
   pruning 36
soil
   condition, checking 38
   deficiencies, rectifying 45
   for container roses 47
   level 38, 39
   neutralizing acid 11
   neutralizing alkaline 11, 24, 45
   preparation 24
   requirements 11
   sterilizing 39
   types 11
specimen Bush roses, pruning 36
spider mite cocktails 44
Spire roses 57, 94, 96, 97, 98, 101
   pruning 36
sports 57-9
spraying 33, 39, 40
square design 21
square walk-about design 20
Standard roses *54*

bud-grafting 59
   pruning 38, *38*
   staking 59
stem canker 46, *46*
stem, definition of 35
striped roses 58
Strydom, Nick 59
summer grooming 31-3
sunburn 46
Sunsation roses 18

T
Taschner, Ludwig 49
Tea roses, origins 60
temperature requirements 11
thrips 39, 43, *43*
trace elements 45
transplanting older roses 26-7

U
Umbrella Standard roses *54*
   training 37
understock, budding on an 28, *28*

V
varieties 56
Victorian rose garden designs 18-23

W
watering
   container roses 47
   roses 11, 30, 38
water
   lack of 30
   quality of 30
weather conditions, extreme 46
white, symbolic value of 12
whitefly 43
winter pruning 34-9

Y
yellow, symbolic value of 12